Crossroads

Crossroads:

Essays on the Catholic Novelists

by

Albert Sonnenfeld

French Literature Publications Company
York, South Carolina

For Mark and Carole

To the Memory of Reinhard Kuhn (1930-1980)

Acknowledgements

I am grateful to the National Endowment for the Humanities and to Princeton University for generous support during 1977-1978, which allowed me the time, while pursuing new research, to review, to revise and to assemble these essays for publication in book form. I am also indebted to the *Princeton University Committee on Research in the Humanities and Social Sciences* for their subvention. Some of these essays have appeared, albeit in somewhat different form: the chapter on Graham Greene is reprinted by permission of the publisher from *The Vision Obscured* by Melvin Friedman (ed.) (New York: Fordham University Press, 1970, pp. 109-128); the chapter on Böll originally appeared, in shorter version, as "They that have not heard shall understand: A study of Heinrich Böll," in *The Shapeless God*, University of Pittsburgh Press, 1968; used by permission. I am also grateful for the generosity of the following in allowing me to incorporate previously published materials: *The Southern Review, L'Esprit créateur, Renascence, Orbis litterarum, French Studies, Contemporary Literature, Journal of European Studies.*

I take particular pleasure in thanking here those colleagues and friends who, over the years, have read, criticized (and even occasionally praised) my work on Catholic fiction: Victor Brombert, Mary Ann Caws, W. M. Frohock, the late Reinhard Kuhn, A. W. Litz, John L. Logan, Stephen G. Nichols, Neal Oxenhandler, Kimberly Sparks, Karl D. Uitti, Theodore Ziolkowski; and, above all, Edward D. Sullivan. They have given the true meaning to the word colleague.

A. S.
Noël 1980

A Foreword that is also a conclusion

I could have been a saint, but I became a man-of-letters.
Paul Theroux

This book of modest proportions may well be the final conclave
of Catholic novelists, for it constitutes an anticipatory, though possibly premature, elegy for an apparently dying form. There *is* something called the Catholic Novel: it is a novel written by a Catholic,
using Catholicism as his informing mythopoeic structure or gener-
ative symbolic system, and where the principal and decisive issue is
the salvation or damnation of the hero or heroine. *Crime and Punishment* may well be a novel about a murder, about the subversion of
certain traditional Russian ideals by Napoleonic theory, but it is,
above all, as the last paragraph of the epilogue states, "the story of
the gradual regeneration of a soul," of the Lazarus-like resurrection
of Raskolnikov and by extension the spiritual rebirth of Russia herself—*Crime and Punishment* is therefore a "Russian Orthodox novel."
My simpleminded and necessarily preemptive definition is my
response to the very novelists who will be considered here: Bernanos,
Böll, Mauriac and Greene, among others, protested (and methinks
they did protest too much) that they were merely novelists who
happened also to be Catholic. They were wrong, I believe, but ironically they were also, in this and in so many matters, prophetic.

Their prophecy, often strident, at times delightfully satirical,
was of the constant threat of the secularization of society and of
the Church herself. Their disclaimers notwithstanding, they had an
inner dread of becoming novelists who happened also to be Catholic.
That prophecy is now well on the way to fulfillment; the cry of warn-
ing, sounded in so many of the works I shall be studying here (particularly in Chapter I), went unheeded. The inexorable forward march

of History has long since swept aside the hopelessly retrograde historical vision of a Percy or a Bernanos; Vatican II marked the legi-
timization and consecration of a host of modernist longings that
were both a reflection and a cause of the "decline and fall" of that
possibly perverse and reactionary nostalgia which made the Catholic
Novel possible. Flannery O'Connor lamented that the South was not
alienated enough, that it was already becoming more, too much more,
like the rest of the country. The South has by now become "the
Sunbelt"; its preachers are no longer those wild thaumaturges of
O'Connor's fiction but "born-again" media-men, their "mission"
indistinguishable from the *hype* of ministering to Los Angeles sub-
urbanites. The dirge of statistics marks the cadence of decline: the
conference of French bishops at Lourdes in October 1978 heard the
bad news that only 99 priests were ordained in France in 1977; the
34,000 priests under 65 in 1965 had fallen to 27,000 by 1975, and
would be fewer than 18,000 by 1985. "The number of vocations remains stationary at a very low level," lamented Monsignor Fretellière,
Chairman of the Commission for the Clergy and Seminaries (*The
Times,* London, October 31, 1978).

My elegiac preface is not a song of lamentation, for I am
neither a reactionary and romantic would-be aristocrat nor a believer.
I am interested in what has in fact happened to the Catholic novel,
to a Graham Greene or a Heinrich Böll, to name but two of those
treated in this book and who are still with us and writing. Louise
de Vilmorin once proffered the delightful boutade that the only
people still worrying about getting married were the priests. The
spokesman for the Bishops Commission for Public Opinion, Bishop
Jean Padré, pointed to celibacy as the main cause of the exodus from
the priesthood in France (*New York Times,* December 10, 1978).
The same newspaper reports on the archdiocese of Newark, New
Jersey's "Ministry to Divorced Catholics," and its director, a Father
Edgar Holden, explains in Post-Vatican II double-speak:

> "The Church neither condones nor encourages divorces. Divorce is
> recognized as the civic reality that it is, the legal reality that it is.
> The Church considers the people still married in the sight of God.
> In my ministry, I sometimes might urge people to get a divorce for
> the legal or economic factors involved, such as alimony or child
> support, which can only be nailed down civilly, legally."

Luc Estang, known to students of French literature as one of the
first advocates of the novels of Bernanos and for a ringing statement
of faith (*Ce que je crois/What I believe/*) hinted that he had lost the
Pascalian wager on God, in his book about Julian the Apostate
(*L'Apostat*); and in a recent volume of verse he bemoans the emptiness of heaven and hails in its stead (and in his 66th year) the power
of carnal love: "Si Dieu est amour l'amour est dieu". The move from
uncial to minuscule is itself emblematic.

The subject of priestly temptation, whether by *libido sentendi*
or *libido sciendi*, is, as the works of Barbey d'Aurevilly show, a mag-
nificent subject for Catholic fiction. But the subject has quickly become domesticated as priests get married and become ex-priests and
even get divorced and become ex-husbands. Instead of the fierce
inner struggle of a modern St. Anthony against concupiscence, we
are now, likely as not, to have a drama of adulterous temptations
à la John Updike. A splendid paradigm of this new worldliness in
Catholic fiction is Mary Gordon's fine first novel, *Final Payments*
(1978).

On the literal level, *Final Payments* represents the first-person
narrator's attempt to settle accounts (or to settle a score) with the
memories of her all too Catholic girlhood. She had spent the full
measure of young adulthood nursing her invalid father, and now at
last he has died. Isabel has paid her debt: her father had had a stroke
some three weeks after finding her in bed with his favorite student.
She will dismiss Margaret, her father's caretaker, will catch up with
her girlhood friends, who are either separated or groping toward
liberated marriage, by dressing provocatively, by having affairs with
her best friend's philandering husband John, her future employer,
and with Hugh Slade, an improbably hen-pecked veterinarian. When
her liberated life leads to one emotional disaster after another,
Isabel decides to reassume the mantle of a nursing sister. She moves
in with the impossibly unpleasant and tyrannical Margaret, accepting
the hairshirt of insults and servitude, shearing off her hair, getting
fat, until once more she feels that she has made a final payment and
escapes with her friends, who have come as Job's comforters. She
has failed in her self-imposed expiatory challenge to "love the un-
loveable," that is to say, Margaret.

It all sounds terribly familiar: the 1960's novel of self-fulfill-
ment, the eternal return of the prodigal after escape from the family
into the counter-culture; "you can't go home again," though a
nervous breakdown is a good try. But if we move from the literal to
one of Dante's higher levels of abstract, symbolic meaning, *Final Payments* becomes a good deal more interesting as a parable of what has
happened to Catholic fiction. Isabel's father, a professor of medieval
literature at St. Aloysius College, shares a vision of history with the
Catholic novelists in the Bernanos tradition:

> his sympathies were with the Royalists in the French Revolution, the
> South in the Civil War, the Russian czar, the Spanish Fascists. He be-
> lieved that Voltaire and Rousseau could be held (and that God was at
> this very moment holding them) personally responsible for the mess
> of the twentieth century. He believed in hierarchies; he believed that
> truth and beauty could be achieved only by a process of chastening
> and exclusion. One did not look for happiness on earth; there was a
> glory in poverty. He would often talk about the happiness of people
> in the slums, although he had never visited one, and he ignored the
> struggle of his own family against poverty, a struggle that ended in his
> mother's madness (pp. 4-5).

(The critical tone here is a further sign that Isabel is telling her story
retrospectively, after her liberation; at the time of her father's life
and death, she could gain no such detachment.) Small wonder, then,
that above her father's desk hung prints of Thomas More, of St.
Jerome with lion, and that his favorite quotation was from the *Chan-
son de Roland:* "*Chrétiens ont droit; païens ont tort*" (pp. 233-234.)
Isabel will err from the path of right onto the primrose path of
dalliance, as a Catholic novel like *Final Payments* is metamorphosed
from a depiction of the straightlaced hairshirt of Isabel's ascesis as
nursing sister to her father into a conventional novel of adultery. In
the world of the Church Isabel is punished for her youthful sexual
adventures with her father's favorite student by her father's stroke,
leading to years of atonement at the bedisde of the invalid. Superficially liberated by his death, she soon thereafter visits a surrogate
priest, a gynecologist, for her IUD, goes to work for her lover who is
director of a state welfare bureau:

> "It might be as big as Medicare."

Dominic and John simultaneously bowed their heads, as if someone had spoken the name of God (p. 129).

Yet as we shall see in the example of Graham Greene, in novels with little Catholic content, one returns, hoping one last time, to try again:

"What are you standing there for like that?" the profile said. "Have you lost the use of your knees?"
"I only want to talk to you," Castle said.
"You aren't here to talk to me," the profile said. There was a chink-chink-chink. The man had a rosary in his lap and seemed to be using it like a chain of worry beads. "You are here to talk to God."
"No, I'm not. I'm just here to talk."
The priest looked reluctantly round. His eyes were bloodshot. Castle had an impression that he had fallen by a grim coincidence on another victim of loneliness and silence like himself.
"Kneel down, man, what sort of Catholic do you think you are?"
"I'm not a Catholic."
"Then what business have you here?"
"I want to talk, that's all."
"If you want instruction you can leave your name and address at the presbytery."
"I don't want instruction."
"You are wasting my time," the priest said.
"Don't the secrets of the confessional apply to non-Catholics?"
"You should go to a priest of your own Church."
"I haven't got a Church."
"Then I think what you need is a doctor," the priest said. He slammed the shutter to, and Castle left the box. It was an absurd end, he thought to an absurd action (Greene, *The Human Factor*, New York, 1978, pp. 241-242).

The priest's advice echoes that of Father Bournisien to the distressed Emma Bovary in Flaubert's anti-clerical vision; Mary Gordon's Isabel expiates her love affairs by attempting to resume the simulacrum of the conventual life as companion to a tyrannical superior, her father's housekeeper, Margaret Casey; but as Greene's priest has shown: the age of theology has yielded to the age of clinical psychology, the Catholic Novel to the psychological novel. Isabel escapes to what may be a new freedom of sexual fulfillment and self-realization. Yet that very freedom may be an ontological formlessness. Like the dying Catholic novel, Isabel's dying father has an unpleasant and unyielding integrity:

And the image filled me with what, through all the years of my
father's illness I had not finally lost: admiration for his fierceness,
for his absoluteness and the consequent ironies of his considerable
tenderness. For my father was sure: he had faith, he had truth; they
had wired his muscles and made his bones like steel. And if his faith
and his truth had made him arrogant and filled him more with hate
than with love (although he *said* it was the love of God that stirred
him) and if his arguments were spurious and even sometimes wicked,
his life had the grandeur of a great struggle, his mind the endurance
of great Renaissance sculpture (p. 39).

The worldliness of psychological domestication typified by
Final Payments seems a trivial tune compared to the resonant chorus
of socialist acolytes celebrating the Church's (and the Catholic
Novel's) secularization in the struggle for social justice. An ex-priest,
Jean-Claude Barrault, now a best-selling author, reports that "in a
modern, mobile society, people tend to get bored as priests." More
than that, the Catholic worship of the sacredness of poverty yields
to pressures from a rising social conscience. The worker-priest movement of the 1950's moved the priests out of the parish church and
into factories, out of the presbytery and into working-class lodgings,
if not into Communist party cells. Controversial at first (the worker-
priests became the subject of a best-selling Catholic novel by Gilbert
Cesbron, *Les Saints vont en enfer,* in 1952), even censured by Pope
Pius XII, the movement was rehabilitated by Paul VI (a conservative
Pope at that) and is now generally accepted: "Our task is to make
the Church potable for people who live in a world where God is apparently absent," said the Rev. Etienne Chevalier, a 49-year-old
priest who drives a truck for a pastry factory (New York *Times,*
December 10, 1978). A paradigm for the newly socialized "Catholic"
novel is a Renaudot prize-winner, *L'Herbe à brûler,* by Conrad
Detrez (1978), the story of a young idealist from the countryside,
who,after studies in a seminary wracked by the controversies of the
time, leaves for Brazil to become a *guerilla* in the Ché Guevara mode,
returning to France only to join the student uprising in 1968. The
1968 meeting of the Latin-American bishops proclaimed that to
enact the Gospel means to "struggle for the liberation of the people
under the yoke of oppression" *(Le Figaro,* October 7, 1978). As epigraph to his novel, *The Honorary Consul,* (1973), Graham Greene
chose a tell-tale remark by Thomas Hardy: "All things merge into
one another— good into evil, generosity into justice, religion into
politics."

"Religion into politics": what was for centuries an indissoluble link now becomes something more than that, a transformation, a substitution. As Dr. Magiot says, in Greene's *The Comedians* (1965), ". . . if you have abandoned faith, do not abandon all faith. There is always an alternative to the faith we lose. Or is it the same faith under another mask?" (p. 308). Though Heinrich Böll has   neither lost his faith nor found another, he has lost his faith in the novel of faith: his great talents as social satirist, always lurking just below the surface of such masterful novels as *Billiard um Halb-Zehn/Billiards at Half-Past Nine/*(1959) and *Ansicht eines Clowns/The Clown/*(1963) (see my chapter V, esp. pp. 115-119) have arisen to become the dominating shapers of his imagination in *Gruppenbild mit Dame/Group Portrait with Lady/*(1971) and *Die verlorene Ehre der Katharina Blum/The Lost Honor of Katharina Blum/*(1974). The excessively compassionate Böll, who lets his better intentions get the worst of him, has taken up "reportorial obligations" (his phrase in *The Lost Honor. . .*), investigating the murder of a journalist in a vast panorama of social corruption or in the even more ambitious polyphonic or kaleidoscopic depiction of Leni Pfeiffer, who had (like Gide's Amédée) become a veritable crossraods where German society of the last fifty years interacts. The tone of both narrations is mordant, particularly with regard to the Church. To the police state techniques of wire-tapping and snooping to entrap Katharina, the Church remains indifferent:

> Has the Bishops' Conference at Fulda or the Executive Committee of German Catholics no ideas on the subject? Why does the Pope keep silent? Does no one realize all the things that assail innocent ears, ranging from *crème brûlée* to hardest porn? We see young people being encouraged to enter the civil service—and to what are they exposed? To moral outcasts of the telephone. Here at last we have an area where church and trade union might cooperate. (*The Lost Honor of Katharina Blum, p. 103*).

The Church as an institution of bureaucratic Pharisees had, of course, always borne the brunt of satire in Catholic fiction whether by Böll (*Murke's Collected Silences*) or by Bernanos (even in the *Diary of a Country Priest* with the Doyen de Blangermont). But here the Church has become *only* an institution, like a trade union or political party. Just a few years earlier, in *Group Portrait with Lady*, there had been a momentary lyric respite to the dazzling satire in the

nostalgic evocation of a still spiritual Catholic, Sister Rahel Maria
Ginzburg, a kind of Simone Weil figure, who converted in 1922,
after a war-time as a socialist pacifist, and entered the convent.
From her grave, as though in memory of a world of belief now closed
to Catholics and open only to the consummate outsider, a Jewish
convert who before conversion "practiced medicine in working-class
areas"; from her grave, springs a miraculous rose:

> The bad part of the Ginzburg case is not, as you might suppose,
> that miracles are being contrived. On the contrary: we can't get rid
> of the miracles. We can't get rid of the roses that bloom where Sister
> Rahel is buried. I admit I have prevented you from talking to Sister
> Cecilia and Scheukens . . . but not because we are manipulating a mir-
> acle, rather because the miracle is manipulating us, and we want to
> keep news-hungry outsiders away from it, not because we desire the
> beatification process but because we don't!

Thus speaks Sister Klementina to the investigating "Au.", as he is
called throughout the novel of factual inquiry.

Graham Greene has become far more overtly political; *he*
selected that Hardy epigraph, and it describes his evolution quite
literally. *The Quiet American* (1955) marks a kind of transition between Greene's explicitly Catholic novels (treated in my Chapter VI)
and his most recent fiction, *The Comedians, The Honorary Consul,
The Human Factor.* Fascinated and repelled by the idea of a Pascalian
wager for God and risk-taking as exemplified by a copy of the *Pen-
sées* on the desk of the police inspector Vigot ("You would have
made a good priest"), the detached and skeptical narrator, the doubting Thomas Fowler, becomes "involved" in love and in an ill-defined
"religion" that comes to him through revulsion at the physical suffering caused by the well-intentioned "crusader for democracy," the
Quiet American, Alden Pyle. Fowler causes Pyle's death, though
whether it has been through possessive jealousy (Pyle had "taken"
Fowler's Vietnamese mistress) or by conviction is deliberately left
unclear. And somehow the politics or the religion of involvement
transforms Fowler's life into a pulp novel with a happy ending: he
gets the girl, his wife finally agrees to a divorce, and the world has
received a demonstration that American innocence is a form of insanity. The narrator of *The Comedians* is similarly detached, yet he

too becomes involved: with his mistress Martha, with the communist rebels against the tyrannical Haitian régime of Papa Doc, with the new political religion embodied by Dr. Magiot. His name is Brown, not Greene, though both are Catholic, as the author points out in the prefatory letter of dedication. He is, as his mistress puts it, *un prêtre manqué*. Trained by the Jesuits, his faith, like that expressed in Greene's Catholic novels, was, under God's shadow, a "very serious affair." "I saw him incarnated in every tragedy." But now he views the mechanism of life as "driven by an authoritative practical joker towards the extreme point of comedy" (pp. 27-28). In the infinite corruption of Duvalier's Haiti, Brown despises all signs of conventionalized belief: the name of Martha's son, the repugnant and sickly Angel, is "a kind of blasphemy" (p. 90); the American presidential candidate Smith's belief in vegetarianism in the struggle against acidity as the cause of passionate excess (Smith is a teetotaler and eats only Yeastrol, as Pyle ate the sandwich spread "Vit-Health"). Brown is far more drawn to the ambiguous Jones, whose world is divided into "Toffs" (those with jobs) and "Tarts" (those who scrounge an uncertain living). But the one prophetic voice in the novel is that of Dr. Magiot, and it is with his "letter from the dead" that the book will end:

> But Communism, my friend, is more than Marxism, just as Catholicism—remember I was born a Catholic too—is more than the Roman Curia. There is a *mystique* as well as a *politique*. We are humanists, you and I. You won't admit it perhaps, but you are the son of your mother and you once took that dangerous journey which we all have to take before the end. Catholics and Communists have committed great crimes, but at least they have not stood aside, like an established society and been indifferent. I would rather have blood on my hands than water like Pilate. . . . if you have abandoned one faith, do not abandon all faith. There is always an alternative to the faith we lose. Or is it the same faith under another mask? (pp. 307-308).

Brown remembers the phrase "prêtre manqué," thinking that he had left involvement behind like the roulette-token he had once dropped in the offertory of the College of the Visitation. But the telephone call from the business entrepreneur, Mr. Fernandez, which awakens Brown from fitful dreams of Jones and summons him "to [his] first assignment" may refer to a future assignment of commitment in memory of Dr. Magiot, killed, in the official Duvalier version, resisting arrest as a Communist agent of Fidel Castro.

The alternative faith of Dr. Magiot comes to life in Leon (Father Leon Rivas), a former priest turned revolutionary. He is the emblem for the evolution of Greene's own literary imagination, as he hints obliquely to the novel's protagonist, Dr. Eduardo Plarr: "There is no room in our packs for books of theology. Only Marta has kept a missal. I have lost mine. Sometimes I have been able to find a paperback novel—like the one I have been reading. A detective story" (*The Honorary Consul*, p. 261). In a detective story, we know what the end will be: "There were no detective stories in the age of faith—God used to be the only detective when people believed in him" (p. 238). *The Honorary Consul* has its detective, Colonel Perez, its gang of criminals, the rebel gang led by Leon ("In a wrong society the criminals are the honest men," p. 114); but the novel is more like a deliberately "bad" thriller with a shootout on the final pages. The rebels wanted to kidnap the American to hold as hostage until the liberation of certain political prisoners held by the government; instead they got Charley Fortnum, a semi-alcoholic English Catholic who more or less appointed himself as "honorary consul," a strictly unofficial and honorific function as greeter of visiting British nationals, but which allows him duty-free importation of foreign automobiles and enormous profits on resale. Throughout the narrative of Fortnum's captivity, the rebel leader Leon betrays his "lost" *vocatus*: "You still talk like a priest, Leon," his former school-mate, Dr. Eduardo Plarr says. "What made you marry?" "I married when I lost faith. A man must have something to guard" is the reply (p. 113). Leon might have given the same reply to the question: "Why are you a revolutionary?" Rivas' wife cannot help but call him "Father"; Fortnum even notices the priestly gesture when Leon makes an omelette:

> "But once a priest always a priest, Father. I spotted you when you broke those eggs over the dish. I could see you at the altar" (p. 124).

In *The Power and the Glory*, Greene had treated the irretrievable permanence of the sacerdotal function: a married whiskey priest but a priest nonetheless, able to give absolution to a dying American gangster. Here the authentic Church seems to have gone underground to become a tentative, if not bumbling, revolutionary cell. But the central focus of the novel is the transformation of Dr. Plarr from indifference and non-involvement. How 19th century of Greene to make his skeptical and detached protagonist a doctor! In any event, with a strangely vague suspicion that his own father may still be alive as a revolutionary in exile, Plarr is more or less coerced into going to the hiding-place of the rebels to care for the injured Fortnum. Like Brown in *The Comedians,* he has a mistress (Fortnum's wife, a former prostitute); he, too, has lost his faith: "I am not a Christian any longer, Leon. I don't think in those terms. I have no conscience. I am a simple man" (p. 207). Plarr will reacquire a conscience, when the hideout is surrounded by Perez' policemen and Plarr crawls out to negotiate with Perez to save the lives both of Fortnum and his captors. Leon follows Plarr: "I thought you might need me." Need as priest at a moment of danger? or as fighting comrade? Then, mysteriously, in a strange but meaningful reversal, Plarr hears Leon's voice addressing him as "Father," as the shots rain forth. In trying to save the others, the skeptical doctor becomes a "priest", and as Leon whispers the words of the penitent: "I am sorry . . . I beg pardon," Plarr, in a flash of memory of schoolboy days, answers: *Ego te absolvo* (p. 291), one of the "unmeaning formulas the priests taught them to use."

If the transformation of priest into revolutionary and intellectual doubter into a "priest" of the revolution sounds familiar, it is because for a moment Greene is rejoining what now might be called an earlier, more naive, left-wing sentimentalism. In Ignazio Silone's *Bread and Wine,* for example, the Church has been irremediably corrupted by its association with Mussolini's fascism. And the worthy priest, Don Benedetto, dies when his communion wine has been poisoned. His student, Pietro Spina, will take on another allegorical name, Paolo Speda, and become the leader of the new underground Church in the catacombs of revolutionary conspiracy. In Kazanzakis' *The Greek Passion,* where the villagers playing parts in a Passion play begin to "live" their parts, "Jesus" becomes an activist, joining the impoverished on the firing-line in a revolution against the greedy land-owners.

But Graham Greene is far too world-weary and disabused to develop the vision of the Revolution as the new, glorious Marxist Church of the dispossessed. Plarr achieves his "salvation" just before his death by becoming involved, not by ideological conversion to the cause. Greene refuses the simple allegorization of the Silone of *Bread and Wine* by willful negation: the one truly evil figure in his recent *The Human Factor* is named *Emmanuel Percival* (sic), a doctor who poisons peanuts to punish a possibly disloyal agent! The lesson of *The Human Factor* is in the title: a priestly imagery is accorded those who are endowed with a human factor, not with ideology: Carson, the South African Communist, had helped Castle and his black wife Sarah to escape. Castle likens him to one of the good priests who worked among the poor in Soweto: "If all priests had been like they were and I had seen them often enough, perhaps I would have swallowed the Resurrection, the Virgin birth, Lazarus, the whole works. . . . For a while I half believed in his (the good priest), like I half believed in Carson's. Perhaps I was born to be a half believer" (p. 140). It is in honor of Carson and in gratitude that Castle becomes a spy; it is a human, not an ideological, obligation. And his bibulous colleague Davis says to him before the Doctor's poison takes effect:

> "You take risks—like they say priests have to do. If I really leaked something—without meaning to, of course—I'd come to you for confession."
> "Expecting absolution?"
> "No. But expecting a bit of justice."
> "Then you'd be wrong, Davis. I haven't the faintest idea what the word 'justice' means."
> "So you'd condemn me to be shot at dawn?"
> "Oh no. I would always absolve the people I liked."
> "Why, then it's you who are the real security risk," Davis said. (p. 171).

Castle is disloyal to his country, but humanly loyal to his wife and her black son (whom he "makes" his flesh-and-blood). And in this higher loyalty he can be likened to a priest (the only priest we meet in *The Human Factor* is the one who tells Castle to see a doctor, and the only doctor we meet is Emmanuel Percival!). The Communist Heng tells Fowler, in *The Quiet American:* "One has to take sides—if one is to remain human." For Greene, as indeed for Böll, involvement used to mean an involvement in the strategy of salvation, taking the Pascalian risk. For both, the spiritual has become humanized, secularized, if one will. The Catholic image has lost its literality; the "Real Presence" has become unreal, a network of imagery. The Catholic novel becomes a novel using Catholic allusions, and Greene can call himself "a Catholic atheist" (New York *Times Magazine*, Feb. 26, 1978, p. 33.). But as "Father" Leon Rivas says: "There is only one way any of us can leave the Church and that is to die" (p. 228).

The essays that make up this book were written over a period of years. They form a kaleidoscopic portrait of the major Catholic novelists of the last fifty years. The book constitutes an elegy to what I perceive as a dying form in a time of radical change for the Church and for those who saw the drama of Catholic salvation as material for modern fiction. Miss Jean Brodie is no longer in her prime. It is my hope that even from without one can sense the power, if not the glory, of the stained-glass window. Certainly, even *extra muros*, one can see the traces of narrative pattern. I would not pretend that the Catholic novel as a sub-genre is an object worthy of purely aesthetic contemplation, but like Isabel's unregenerately reactionary or anachronistic father, the Catholic novel can be seen as arrogant, often filled more with hate than with love. And if its arguments are spurious and even sometimes wicked, it has the "grandeur of a great struggle and the endurance of great Renaissance sculpture."

Princeton University
January 1981

Chapter I

Don Quixote and the Romantic Reactionaries

> Men have left GOD not for other gods, they say, but for
>   no god; and this has never happened before
> That men both deny gods and worship gods, professing
>   first Reason
> And then Money, and Power, and what they call Life or
>   Race, or Dialectic.
>
> T. S. Eliot: *The Rock*

The Catholic novel flowers only in desecrated soil. Like the
Counter-Reformation, it is reactionary: a frightened look at the mor-
bid anarchy of modern life, then a bitter denunciation of the degenerate kingdom of this world. In his ill-conceived pilgrimage to the
gilded shrines of the apostate goddess of progress, modern man, we
are told repeatedly, has not only misread all the sign-posts and taken
all the wrong turns, he has made the very landscape of his striving
into formless wasteland. Scientific evolution had taught man to think
that "so long as they were passing from the ape they were going on,"
Chesterton noted; "but you can pass from the ape and go to the
devil." To retrace one's steps seems historically impossible, despite
the deluded hopes of the Council of Trent, French advocates of the
Restoration, Franco's *Falange*. The past cannot be recaptured;
it can only be reimagined, for, having taken place, the past has
achieved the formal immutability (or perfection) of art. One thinks
of the meditations of Thomas Mann's historian, Professor Cornelius
(in *Disorder and Early Sorrow*), for whom the disorder of 16th century Spain has become very orderly indeed because it has moved

from being to inscription in the historians' archives. The Church cannot herself legislate a return to a status quo ante. *Ante* what: Ante-Reformation? Ante-Crucifixion? Ante-Original Sin?

It was as poets and dreamers that Catholic novelists viewed history, transmitting a vision, a memory of a story-book past that was surely never as glorious as their nostalgia intimated—that much, history can objectively prove in refutation of Bernanos' apotheosis of 12th century Christian knights. But more than from simple romantic nostalgia, the great ages of belief, of significant forms, attain their luster from the wishful thinking of the creators of imaginative literature, not from the dry facts of history. And while they sustained their belief in an ill-defined golden age where Christianity was synonymous with civilization, as Novalis puts it in *Christianity or Europe*, our quixotic reactionaries went on denouncing and satirizing the excesses of the present and the threats of the future. When one of the good sisters busily counting the Church receipts (in J. F. Power's story, *The Lord's Day*), mistakenly refers to a young Irish priest as "Father O'Mammon of St. Judas' parish," she is merely echoing a refrain which sounds the Catholic novelist's disdain for our new 'age of gold.' When at the end of her labors she hurries to a sink "to wash the money off her hands," she is emblematic of the ablutionary exorcisms performed by our novelists' on a world fallen from grace.

The Catholic novel thrives on the Church's adversity, and it should come as no surprise to find the roots of Catholic fiction in France, the country that had once been, in Léon Bloy's words, "the beloved elder daughter of the Church," but was now "the slut of the world" ["la salope du monde"]. The French Revolution had unleashed and then consecrated in a position of power precisely those social forces which were to become the objects of our Catholic novelists' wrath not only in France, but in Europe generally: belief in progress, the secularization of society, the capitalistic profit motive, middle-class egalitarianism. After 1789, a horde of substitute religions overran the already profaned temple—gold replaced God, science deposed mystery, Rousseau's corporate will threatened to make the hero obsolete, and reason (and raison d'état) destroyed Faith (and regional autonomy). New allegories replaced the old. During the weeks of Lent in the Siberian prison camp, Dostoevsky's Raskolnikov dreams of a terrible, unknown plague. The new germs which lodged in the bodies of men were endowed with reason and will, but strangely the plague-ridden considered themselves infinitely wise, raising armies to defend a truth which resided only on their side: "Wholesale destruction stalked the earth." The plague is, of course, Dostoevsky's mythical rendering of the infestation of Russia by rationalism and atheism, synonymous for him with Raskolnikov's poisonous theory of the extraordinary Napoleonic man. [Dostoevsky himself, needless to say, was a vociferous enemy of the Roman Church, but his imaginative patterns, his disdain for progress and nostalgia for an earlier agrarian, even feudal, age, so directly anticipate the obsessions of many of our Catholic novelists that Bernanos, as we shall see in detail, announced his ambition to "rewrite Dostoevsky but within a Catholic mode or framework."] And these plagues of new beliefs had their origins in France, though in the wake of the Napoleonic wars and their sequels they were to spread throughout Europe. Angry Catholic voices sounded a continuous and angry protest. Ernest Hello attacked *M. Renan, Germany and Atheism in the 19th century;* Hilaire Belloc described the doubtful blessings of *The Servile State* (1912), while his friend G. K. Chesterton wondered *What's wrong with the world?* (1910). Léon Bloy's self-proclaimed vocation as *An Entrepreneur of Demolitions* (1884) was echoed by later demolitions experts like Georges Bernanos *(France against the Robots,* 1944) and Julien Green *(Pamphlet against French Catholics,* 1927). The titles are telltale. Many Catholic novelists (one could add Barbey d'Aurevilly, Sigrid Unset and Evelyn Waugh) felt the need to do direct battle with the enemy in newspapers and magazines. Belloc was to explain the widespread Catholic bellicosity this way in his essay, *The Counter Attack through History:*

> I ought, perhaps, to have called this essay "The Apologetic from History." I prefer the more provocative title, because it is the more true. There is a permanent general need for an apologetic drawn from history; but there is particular need, urgent at the present moment, for a counter-attack upon the false history which has been used to undermine the Catholic faith in the minds of men, to shake the confidence of Catholics in themselves, or to confirm in error those who are brought up in error.

The point is that though the above-named counterinsurgents are among the most distinguished creators of Catholic fiction, their talents were initially negative or reactionary. *Their inspiration increases when the Church's power decreases; they thirst most acutely for a world of order when their world is threatened by total disorder; and they consistently confuse history with theology.*

In those countries where belief and Catholic preeminence had not been decimated by the dissolution of traditional social structures, the Catholic novelist, with his basic initial impulse of counterattack, has not yet displaced the Catholic apologist or hagiographer. Thus there have as yet been few Spanish, Italian or Irish novels of the type created by Bernanos, Graham Greene or Elisabeth Langgässer. And when in those landscapes of continuing belief "Catholic novels" do materialize, it seems to be when the Church is threatened. Thus, Ricardo Leon's now unreadable novels accompanied the Carlist movement in Spain in the 1870's; the turn-of-the-century controversy about modernism in the Italian Church inspired Fogazzaro's famous *The Saint*. More recently, the modernization of previously theocratic Québec after the virtual 'reign' of Maurice Duplessis seems to be arousing some Catholic counterattacks imitated from the French polemicist tradition of Bernanos and Mauriac (I think of Langevin's *The Time of Men* and *The Burden of God* by Gilles Marcotte). Those are countries, along with much of the Latin America of the past, where the pre-industrial agrarian social structure had retained, until recently, much of its integrity; there, too, the temporal as well as spiritual ascendency of the Church had rarely encountered serious literary challenge. In contrast, one need only look at the picture in France at the time of the first wave of Catholic novels, from Barbey d'Aurevilly's *The Bewitched Woman [L'Ensorcelée]* (1854) to Huysmans' *The Oblate [L'Oblat]* (1903). The calendar of Church-State relations of that half-century is reminiscent of the 1790-1801 period: constant harassment, even physical intimidation, of Church orders, culminating in Gambetta's famous declaration of war on clericalism in 1878, was followed by the passage of a block of anti-Church legislation that ranged from the education bills of 1886 to the separation of Church-and-State law of 1905. ("A Day of mourning!" was proclaimed by the Catholic newspaper, *La Croix*.) There was even a wave of clerical emigration to more salubrious climes (recalling 1791) as a result of the associations bill of 1901. All the while, the very structure of French society was threatened by the Franco-Prussian War, by the subsequent Communes, and finally by the protracted Dreyfus case which once again, in its final resolution, seemed to readers of *La Croix* an historic Jewish-Masonic plot. It was clearly a time for counterattack, rather than homily. The second wave of French Catholic novels, those of Bernanos, Mauriac and Julien Green, is similarly a response to a crisis in the traditional order of faith and society. World War I and the Bolshevik Revolution gave Catholic Europe a sense of imminent Apocalypse: "I really believe that my book is one of the books born from the war," Bernanos said of his first novel, *The Star of Satan [Sous le Soleil de Satan]* (1926), though the war is not mentioned within the novel itself. For him, the months of boredom in the trenches symbolized the desanctification of heroism in an impersonal industrial age. The sense of risk and Christian honor of "the poor horseman who had only his cape and sword" seemed a pitiful anachronism now. (One thinks of the *St.-Cyriens* in full cavalry regalia charging the mechanized German forces in 1914.) Such Catholic writers as Psichari (*The Call to Arms [L'Appel des armes]*, 1913) and Charles Péguy tried to resurrect the warrior spirit of Joan of Arc and died on the front. But it was the carnival atmosphere of post-Armistice Paris that proved the degeneracy of the age. "Disappointment forced me into literature," Bernanos explained in *France against the Robots [La France contre les robots]*, evoking Paris as bordello. A vortex of godless pleasure-seekers moves convulsively through many Catholic novels of the time [in Mauriac's *Evil* (*Le Mal*, 1924) and *The Desert of Love* (*Le Désert de l'amour,*1925), in Julien Green's *Derelicts* (*Epaves*, 1932]* as though to illustrate Pascal's famous Pensée on boredom: "Nothing is so unbearable to man than to be fully at rest, without passions, without business, without distractions. . ." Julien Green echoes Pascal in his Journal for 1938:

> If I ever undertook to convert someone—which Heaven forbid— churches would not be the places to which I should take him. No, it would be to those so-called places of pleasure. For nothing is more melancholy, nothing confers a greater longing for the Absolute than to see men and women dancing to the accompaniment of the howls and groans of a negro band, amid clouds of cigarette smoke and the heat of an overcrowded room. This spurious imitation of happiness

is so ugly and so sad that it is enough to make one long to leave
this world forever and ever.

In England, the Church's tribulations in modern times are no
doubt less dramatic than in France, but you would hardly know that
from the reactions of a Hilaire Belloc to the anomalies of the Education Bill of 1906: "since Diocletian nothing can compare with the
persecution of the Catholic people of this country by the wealthy
and official classes. It has not been a popular persecution, but a cold,
deliberate and bloody persecution on the part of the men who got
hold of the land of the country after the dissolution of the monas-
teries." This in the land of the Catholic Relief Acts! The very minority
status of the Church was of itself sufficient cause for the aggressive
pamphleteering of the Francophile Belloc (*An Open Letter on the
Decay of Faith,* 1906) and the proselyte G. K. Chesterton (*Orthodoxy,*
1908), but the most efficient irritant was the capitalist profit motive
in the age of the new gold: "Our civilisation/Is built on coal/ Our
civilisation/That lump of damnation/Without any soul. . ." The *dis-
tributism* of "Chesterbelloc" (as Shaw called the pair) was supposed
to provide an antidote to statism and to prevent future Marconi
scandals by encouraging small property owners and artisans. Evelyn
Waugh and Graham Greene are contemporaries (born in 1904), and
their Catholic novels were shaped by the dissolution of religious
values brought on by the jazz age and climaxed by World War II.
With his epigrammatic brilliance, Waugh was clearly the successor to
Chesterton, and like him reacted against the imminent collapse of
the revered social hierarchy even before his conversion (indeed the
impulse for that conversion might be said to be linked to his snobbish
yearning for aristocracy). In a scene which for Waugh is emblematic
of the total despiritualization of the age of "the bright young things,"
a customs inspector (in Waugh's novel *Vile Bodies,* 1930) confiscates
a copy of the Dante's *Purgatorio,* explaining: "French, eh? I guessed
as much, and pretty dirty, too, I shouldn't wonder." Yet Waugh's
properly Catholic novels were written later, in response to the more
radical upheaval during World War II: *Brideshead Revisited* (1945),
Helena (1950), *Men at War,* also called the "Guy Crouchback trilogy"
(1952-63). While Waugh's fellow convert, Graham Greene, never
shared in reactionary political nostalgia for an agrarian feudal society, he too is coming to grips with a world in disintegration: "One

feels at home in London or in Liverpool or Bristol or any of the bombed cities, because life there is what it ought to be. If a cracked cup is put in boiling water it breaks, and an old dog-toothed civilisation is breaking now." Greene's Catholic fiction was written under the spell of Mauriac's gloomy talent. *Brighton Rock* (1938) depicts the vice-ridden sensation seekers of Mauriac's *The Dark Angels (Les Anges noirs)*. Greene's most parochial novels, *The Power and the Glory* (1940); *The Heart of the Matter* (1948) and *The End of the Affair* (1951) were, as we shall see, written *in extremis,* within sight of the *Apocalypse* of atheistic socialism, British colonialism, German aerial bombardments.

The destruction of the traditional order in Germany itself is even more dramatic, of course, what with two disastrous world wars separated by the economic collapse of the 1920's and the rise of National Socialism. Here, as in England, the practitioners of Catholic fiction were often converts, who keenly felt their recently acquired minority status. Gertrud von Le Fort converted in 1918, wrote her first major novel, *The Roman Fountain [Der Römische Brunnen]* in 1928 to describe her conversion, but revealingly waited almost twenty years to complete its sequel, *The Angels' Crown [Der Kranz der Engel]*, (1946), a work that despite its post-World War I setting was obviously shaped by the horrors of the Nazi period. Many of Mme. von Le Fort's historical novels, *The Last to the Scaffold [Die Letzte am Schafott]* (1931) and *The Magdeburg Wedding [Die Magdeburgische Hochzeit]* (1938), to name but two, represent attempts to treat the disintegration of our own times in terms of earlier historical crises. Elisabeth Langgässer faces the problem more courageously in *The Indelible Seal [Das Unauslöschliche Siegel]* (1946) and *The Quest [Märkische Argonautenfahrt]* (1950), symbolic chronicles of the perversion of the German spirit from 1914 to 1945. The pilgrimage of the penitent Argonauts to the convent at Anastasiendorf amid the ruins of what *was* Germany mirrors both the expiatory gesture of the novelist herself in writing her book and her longing for the conventual order of the past. "Where were you, Adam? I was in the second World War," the epigraph to one of Heinrich Böll's novels, signals that the fact of war cannot be escaped in all German fiction of the 1940's. But the perception of the War's role in the providential design of history was largely left to such Catholic writers as Stefan Andres (*We are Utopia [Wir sind Utopia]*,

(1942) and Böll himself (*Billiards at Half-Past Nine [Billiard um Halb-Zehn]*, (1959).

I shall also be examining perhaps the leading exponent of American Catholic fiction Flannery O'Connor. It is curious that while the obvious threats of revolutionary persecution of the religious are hardly a major preoccupation and while the notion of a gloriously Catholic Ancien Régime would be an aberration for an American, the few serious practitioners of Catholic fiction fit into the pattern. It may be no accident that Allen Tate, Walker Percy, and O'Connor are Southerners, for in that region of "Agrarian poets", nostalgia for traditional social structures linked to traditional religious structures is somewhat more plausible. In Tate's *The Fathers* (1928), the progressive alienation between generations is magically dissolved for an instant when a rodeo takes on all the traditional glamour of a medieval joust. Flannery O'Connor explains that her Southern and Catholic anguish lies not in isolation from the rest of the country but "by the fact that it [the South] is not alienated enough, that every day we are getting more and more like the rest of the country, that we were being forced out not only of our many sins, but of our few virtues. This may be unholy anguish but it is anguish nevertheless." Among those "few virtues" is the literal belief in Hell of the Fundamentalists who populate her works; O'Connor uses these Johannine extremists, as we shall see, as metaphors for authentic Catholic belief in the literal reality of Satan. The progressive integration of the American Church into the secularized mainstream inspires the satirical pen of the Catholic J. F. Powers (he tells of a virtually computerized rosary one attaches to the steering-wheel, so as to be able to tally one's *Paters* and *Aves* while driving!). But mostly American Catholic fiction has become sentimentalized, has lost the high seriousness of theme and purpose which characterizes even satirical works by the major authors. There has been a plethora of quaint parish-house novels, films, television scripts:

> Even a wise, compassionate priest like Father O'Malley occasionally runs into a puzzler. What, for instance, can you do with a boy who sings like an angel and thinks like a crook? Tonight, Gene Kelly as Father O'Malley tries to explain why one should not put holy medals in parking meters . . . even if they do fit.

I have been dealing here not with history as it was, but with history, as it were, and it is time to assess the meaning of this peculiar concordance of history and fiction. From the very first, the Catholic novelistic vision has often been distorted by a confusion of faith and politics, especially reactionary politics. Though all modern writers can be said to have shared a common historical experience, no group has been consistently more *engagé* than the Catholic writers, but then no religion has been as committed to the exercise of temporal power as the Roman Catholic Church. Barbey d'Aurevilly joined with the die-hard Catholic legitimists in the salon of Madame de Maistre fifteen years before resuming religious practice; Bernanos fought in the streets alongside of the *Camelots du Roi* long before his first novel; as a child, Evelyn Waugh (according to his father's autobiography) dreamed of founding a "pistol troop" to defend England against Germans and Jews. One is led to wonder whether political reaction is an indispensable catalyst for faith. "My theme is memory, that winged host that soared about me one grey morning of war-time," Evelyn Waugh wrote in *Brideshead Revisited*. The Catholic novelist is so often reactionary because he is committed to the past. His novels are essentially criticisms of the progressive dechristianization of a world in crisis. To be sure, he accepts our historical condition as the stuff of which novels must be made. Prayer and celebration belong to poetry (to poetry as prayer, as the Abbé Brémond said); the novel, with its 19th century positivistic antecedents, is of necessity, as we shall see in the next chapter, an instrument of analysis, earthbound, reflecting the mud of life and not the ray of the Divine Diadem. The reader, especially if *Extra muros,* is earthbound too. He can respond to Pascal's thoughts on the misery of man without God, while remaining refractory to the *Mémorial;* he is at home in the *Confessions* of St. Augustine, but an alien intruder in the City of God. He responds to novels, not to hagiography. So too with the Catholic novelist. To communicate he must acknowledge temporal reality, but he does so only to castigate the more virulently those traits which are anathema to him and, he believes, to God. If he reacts to a century of revolution by condemning the republic, by denouncing industrialism, capitalism and science, it is because he views history itself as a symbolic struggle between God and the fallen angel. What makes our Catholic novelists double in violence is the very hopelessness of their cause. They are not only fighting particular enemies of the Faith, but time itself. Another restoration of the monarchy in France, even under the Comte de Chambord's white banner of royalism would not remove the speculators from their columned shrine on the Place de la Bourse; nor could a restoration undo a century of industrialization. Men of letters all, despite their occasional role as political activists, despite their frequent calling as committed journalists, the Catholic novelists militate against the general condition of modern man, rather than against a specific removable political or religious institution. They despise capitalism, but reject socialism; they denounce the self-righteous faithful as much as the republican infidel. What they are ultimately doing is to perform an exorcism on a fallen world. The more deeply engrained the demonic presence, the more violent must be the purge. As undeclared thaumaturges, seeking to end the reign of the "prince of this world" (Bernanos' words), their endless imprecations become nothing less than the ritual formulae of the Inquisitor before the *auto da fé*, the convulsive blows of St. Michael's sword raining down on the hated dragon. And if they give a hint of something better in the past (the Church militant, military and monastic of the Crusades or the preindustrial, agrarian social structure, they are not to be taken literally, for they are vestigial romantics after all. Paul Claudel described the setting of *The Tidings brought to Mary* (*L'Annonce faite à Marie*) as "the end of a stylized Middle Age much the way medieval poets might have imagined Antiquity." Our Catholic novelists (much like Dostoevsky and Solzhenitsyn in Russia) long for the integrity of a period which some of them *call* the Middle Ages. What they ultimately project, however, is an edenic vision: The resurrection of the past implies the eradication of the perplexities of the present; the anarchy of the modern world, where we perceive God only through the shadow He casts, is magically dispelled by a return to consecrated forms.

II

G. K. Chesterton's *Napoleon of Notting Hill* (1904) takes place toward the end of the progressively democratized 20th century. In this mechanized and depersonalized future, the king has become a "universal secretary," the soldiers no longer wear splendid uniforms but are attired "in a sombre and hygienic manner." Suddenly, as though in defiance, a stately man, dressed in a military outfit of brilliant green, appears to perform the fierce gestures of exorcism upon the modern world. He tears a piece of yellow paper from a billboard advertising mustard, stabs his palm with a penknife, soaking up the blood with a borrowed handkerchief, and pins the now crimson handkerchief and the yellow paper side by side on the breast of his uniform. These are the national colors of Nicaragua; the officer is the last nationalist. And while even Nicaragua has been overrun by the brute powers of modernity, the national spirit is not dead, it is an idea! The consequences of the officer's Romantic gesture will be far-reaching. Auberon Quin, a witness to the deed, is named king (King Auberon!). While he is "mingling with his people" one day, he meets a little boy with a wooden sword and a cocked paper hat who strikes him with the sword, proclaiming: "I am the king of the castle!" As a result of these two encounters the king will decree a revival of the "arrogance" of the old medieval cities. Each London borough is to build a city wall, to raise a city guard, to choose a banner, a coat of arms, and a gathering cry. The age of heroism has returned: mammoth battles take place in the streets, and the little boy grows up to become the most valiant of warriors. What started out as a burlesque turns into an epic, Auberon realizes. The toy soldiers in a shop window become icons, witnesses "to that terror and beauty, that desire for a lovely death"; the wooden sword becomes "a magic wand and nothing it touches can be vulgar." At first glance, there would seem to be nothing particularly Catholic about Chesterton's delightful novel, but its pattern of plot is intensely Catholic in its Romantic vision of history.

Instead of ironizing quixotism in *The Return of Don Quixote* (1927), Chesterton mocks the realists. The librarian, Michael Herne, becomes a specialist in the Middle Ages in order to qualify for a part in a play about *Blondel the Troubadour*: "I was looking at an old missal in the library yesterday. You know they always gilt the name of God? I think if they gilt any word now it would be Gold." "Perhaps it is only in childhood that books have any deep influence on our lives," Graham Greene once wrote. Herne's role in the play stands for "boyhood dreams of the past, full of knight errants and hermits and all the rest." But in a Pirandellian fit of madness, Herne refuses to give up playing his role when the curtain falls after his performance; he will not give up the magic of the Middle Ages, continuing to wear his costume and ridiculing modern attire: "My very hood has the shape of a gothic window." Other medievalists join in a charade that threatens to become reality. Rosamund Severne organizes a political party along medieval lines (she had earlier tried to prove that *Paradise Lost* was written by Charles II!); she proclaims a new regime "the League of the Lion," outlawing firearms in favor of bows and arrows. As anarchy threatens England, the beleagered Prime Minister gives power to the medievalists. The librarian becomes King-at-Arms of the West Country; Seawood Abbey, recently a country manor and the scene of the play which gave birth to the new Don Quixote, becomes an Abbey once more. Rosamund converts, entrusting the Abbey to the newly annointed Abbot, Michael Herne:

> "Do you blame us if we have dreamed of a return to simpler things? Do you blame us if we sometimes fancy that a man might not do what all this machinery is doing if hence he were a man and no longer a machine?"

Herne's words echo Chesterton's own:

> How high the sea of human happiness rose in the Middle Ages! We now only know of the colossal walls that they built up to keep it in bounds. How low human happiness sank in the 20th century our children will only know by these extraordinary modern books, which tell people to be cheerful and that life is not so bad after all. Humanity never produces optimists till it has ceased to produce happy men.

In a *Paris Review* interview, Evelyn Waugh said he would have chosen to be born in the 13th century. The old schoolmaster in his *Scott-King's Modern Europe* (1947) tells us that "it would be very wicked indeed to do anything to fit a boy for the modern world."

The dust in *A Handful of Dust* (1934) is what is left of the past. The hero, appropriately (Catholic authors have a nostalgia for allegorical names) christened Tony *Last,* lives in a 19th century Gothic mansion built on the grounds of what used to be Hetton Abbey (compare Seawood in *The Return of Don Quixote).* His financial resources and imaginative energies are devoted solely to the restoration of the mansion's former splendor, a factitious splendor, of course, since the style is imitation Gothic. He wonders, while contemplating the pattern of Tudor roses and fleurs-de-lis (those aristocratic symbols), whether "it would be easy, nowadays, to find a craftsman capable of such delicate work." Tony's love for the house will cost him the affection of his wife Brenda, who runs off with the social upstart, the busy John Beaver. His dream of perpetuating the traditions of the past will lead to the death of his only son, for John Andrew has only a partial mastery of the rudiments of horsemanship and on his first hunt is thrown and trampled when a motorcycle backfires. The mechanical horsepower has made another victim. Tony escapes. He becomes an explorer in quest of a city, the fortified city of the heraldic past:

> It was Gothic in character, all vanes and pinnacles, gargoyles, battlements, groining and tracery, pavillions and terraces, a transfigured Hetton, pennons and banners floating on the sweet breeze ... a coral citadel crowning a green hill-top sewn with daisies.

Tony Last's failure is no less complete than that of the would-be warrior, the Catholic Guy Crouchback, in *Men at Arms, Officers and Gentlemen* and *The End of the Battle.* Last scion of an illustrious Catholic family whose homestead, after being held in uninterrupted succession since the reign of Henry I, was now rented to a convent, Guy Crouchback was living at "Castello Crouchback" in Italy when news of Germany's attack on Czechoslovakia reaches him. He wants a place in that battle and consecrates his intention by praying at the tomb of one "Roger of Waybroke, Knight, an Englishman; his arms five falcons. His sword and gauntlet still lay beside him." Sir Roger was a crusader; Guy Crouchback seeks to emulate him by joining the tradition-bound Halberdiers, yet everywhere he is thwarted by the bureaucratic bumbling of the modern army. Even the Church no longer can console; in a confessional in Alexandria the confessor turns out to be a spy who whispers questions about troop movements rather than the usual queries on sin. So great is Guy's frustration at being repeatedly denied a hero's death that he has the following inspiration:

> There should be a drug for soldiers, to put them to sleep until they were needed. They should repose among the briar like the knights of the Sleeping Beauty; they should be laid away in their boxes in the nursery cupboard.

Ernest Psichari was Renan's grandson, but in sounding the *Call to Arms* (1913) and in writing *The Centurion's Voyage* (1916) [*L'Appel des armes* and *Le Voyage du Centurion*], he expressed his ambition to be "a soldier of Christ, *miles Christi.*" His contemporary Charles Péguy sang: "Happy are those who die in great battles!" Only one soldier in Evelyn Waugh's military trilogy attains the beatitude of a Sir Roger. There were no witnesses to the anonymous young Englishman's death, and it is perhaps for this very reason that Crouchback is able, in his mind's eye, to transform the physically undefiled body into an artistic vision:

> The soldier lay like an effigy on a tomb, like Sir Roger in his shadowy shrine at Santa Dulcina . . . . Meanwhile the three of them stood by the body, stiff and mute as figures in a sculptured Deposition.

What is important is that the effigy is timeless and yet embodies the permanent reality of the past in the present. Late in the trilogy, when Crouchback is parachuted behind the German lines to rendezvous with Yugoslav Resistance fighters, he can only communicate in Latin with the Partisans' chaplain: *Miles anglicus sum.* Modern secularization has been dispelled; we have returned to the days of the Crusades, of the Church militant and military.

The same imaginative process leads Charles Ryder (Ritter—Knight), the devotee of the aristocracy who is the narrator of *Brideshead Revisited,* to become an architectural painter. The old houses of England's Catholic nobility live on in his albums: "After my first exhibition," he writes, "I was called to all parts of the country to make portraits of houses that were soon to be deserted or debased; indeed, my arrival seemed often to be only a few paces ahead of the auctioneers, a presage of doom." Though Charles, despite his name, is not an aristocrat, he does come close to marrying the noble Julia. A variation of Ryder's attempt to preserve the past through art can be seen in the family history which Lady Marchmain commissions from the ludicrous Mr. Samgrass. In the past, the Marchmains "lived sequestered lives among their tenantry and kinsmen," but now the nobility are impecunious and degenerate. The Brideshead mansion which gives the novel its name and inspires Ryder's meditation on the past glories and foibles of its owners, was made from stones of what used to be the family castle. Despite this decline, despite the fact that the worthless young aristocrat Sebastian Flyte loves only his own childhood, alcohol, his teddy-bear Aloysius, and his sister's prize-winning pig, Francis Xavier (more or less in that order), Evelyn Waugh intimates that there *was* something holy and beautiful in this Catholic family, and that vestiges of this past remain in that very blue blood. On his deathbed, Lord Marchmain himself tells us that "we were knights then, barons since Agincourt; the later honours came with the Georges." Marchmain's conversion *in extremis* offers an oblique hope that all is not lost.

III

"I am a man of old France, or rather of France, for a thousand years of history cannot be wiped out by 150 years of wretched fumbling." Georges Bernanos is, of course, much less of a snob than Waugh, yet he shares a good measure of the latter's nostalgia for aristocracy and chivalry. For him, a Christian knight of the 12th century seems less out of style than "a bourgeois intellectual." Like Waugh, Bernanos was under the continuing spell of childhood readings and confuses imaginative literature with historical possibilities. He wrote, in 1928, to the Count of Paris, the pretender to the French throne:

> With you, whenever you want, we shall make history! And what
> history! The kind which three or four centuries later becomes a

saga, a fine novel of adventure with illustrations in color that make girls dream and little boys shout for joy.

Despite Bernanos' self-proclaimed status as "a man of Old France," the aristocrats who populate his novels are every bit as decrepit as Waugh's. The Marquis de Cadignan in *The Star of Satan* is unmarried and the last member of his family. His energies are devoted to a vain attempt to revive the lost art of falconry; failing which, he becomes a hunter of flesh, mostly female, a pastime that leads to his murder. His chateau is soon to be sold at auction. The neurasthenic, if blue-blooded, Monsieur de Clergerie, in *Joy (La Joie)* "had the honor of belonging to the Academy of Moral Sciences, and was now maneuvering to become a member of *the* Academy . . ." One could read "twelve boring volumes inscribed on his narrow face." Monsieur le Comte, in *Diary of a Country Priest (Journal d'un curé de campagne),* is involved in a sordid love affair with his daughter's governess. Characteristically, *his* only son had died. "There's no longer any aristocracy," one of the count's own relatives tells the Curé. "No family can hold out against the slow sapping process of greed, when the law is the same for everyone, and public opinion the standard. The aristocrats of today are only shame-faced *bourgeois.*" In *M. Ouine,* Bernanos' gloomiest novel, Madame de Néreis, the chatelaine, is insane and a nymphomaniac. An auto-da-fé is called for:

> That damn chateau, those damn castellans. Fire, do you hear me?
> Fire, that's what one would need to finish with that nest of frogs
> and lies. A fine fire, damn it! and for the castellan, a hair shirt, as
> in the times of the monks! . . .

We shall see hairshirts aplenty later. Here I want only to insist that like Waugh, Bernanos remains paradoxically convinced that the aristocracy *can* erect its own barriers against the sea of boredom which is engulfing modern man. His Royalist politics attest to that, of course; and we shall see that Romantic nostalgia is a secret determinant in his enthusiastic backing of, and identification with, General De Gaulle and Free France.

The clearest emblematic figuration of Georges Bernanos as quixotic reactionary is a romantic and beautiful scene in *Diary of a Country Priest.* The ailing priest meets Olivier, the nephew of the despair-ridden Countess. He had been sent away to exile in the Foreign Legion at eighteen because he was so rebellious and difficult. Olivier, whose name is that of one of the heroes of the *Song of Roland,* roars into the book on a motorcycle. (The motorcycle is one of Bernanos' personal symbols of daring and adventure; it is the equivalent here of the rearing stallion of a crusador.) "The crest in front of me," writes the Curé, "became as though crowned with sprouting flames—the sun was beating down hard on the polished steel." The brilliant lighting of this scene is in striking contrast to the endless mud and rain (obsessively recurring symbols of boredom and evil for the author) which constitute the decor of the northern parish of Ambricourt. Olivier takes the Curé for a brief ride, and during those few hair-raising moments the priest learns the joys of youth, the exhilaration of spiritual and physical risk. Olivier is the embodiment of Péguy's soldier: a Christian knight and the "last" soldier, though Olivier himself insists that the last real soldier died in 1431, burned at the stake by the Church herself. The titulary gods of today are called bankers, Olivier maintains; Christianity died with the secularization of the soldier. In a revealingly analogous image (taken from Graham Greene's *A Burnt-out Case* (1960), the open khaki shirt and trim pointed beard of one of the young jungle priests whom Querry meets in Africa remind him of a young officer in the Foreign Legion "whose recklessness and ill-discipline had led to an heroic and wasteful death," Olivier also wants to die young.

> When a man has found something which he prefers to life, he then for the first time begins to live . . . . When once he has despised this world as a mere instrument, it becomes a musical instrument, it falls into certain artistic harmonies around him.

Those could be the words of Olivier; they come instead from Chesterton's essay, *On Heroes.*

IV

Bernanos was proud to have dreamed of saints and of heroes, neglecting "the intermediate forms of our species." The venality of the bourgeois, the *embourgeoisement* of the aristocrats, the seculari-zation of the modern Church herself and the Pharisaism of the faith-ful have lead our Catholic romantics to idealize the asceticism and self-mortification of the medieval monks and hermits, and beyond that the integrity of the persecuted underground Church. These Catholic novelists, writing *inter muros,* are among the severest critics of the Church hierarchy (and among the most pungent satirists of Catholic foibles). Invariably, their novels abound in caricatural Church officials and hypocritical pious ladies. One need only name a few: Mauriac's *Woman of the Pharisees (La Pharisienne)* or Isa in *Vipers Tangle (Le Noeud de Vipères);* Mme Plasse in Julien Green's *The Visionary (Le Visionnaire);* Mr. Rycker in *A Burnt-out Case,* and Louise Scobie in *The Heart of the Matter.* Among the cloth, the luke-warm, intermediate forms of the species abound: the Dean of Blangermont in the *Diary of a Country Priest;* Don Giovanni Moro-sini in Carlo Coccioli's *The White Stone (Le Caillou blanc),* and the excessively indulgent and onomastically venal Father Rothschild, S. J. (!) of Waugh's *Vile Bodies.* The Church has her own bourgeoisie, we soon learn. Or as Querry puts it in *A Burnt-out Case:*

> Those who marry God can become domesticated too—it's just as humdrum a marriage as all the others . . . . it was God's taste to be worshipped and their taste to worship, but only at stated hours like a suburban embrace on a Saturday night.

"For Bernanos, the monk becomes a village priest," the perceptive Jesuit critic, André Blanchet, once wrote. Like Alyosha Karamazov, the priest-heroes of a Bernanos and a Coccioli are constantly asking to be returned to the monastery. Those who win our author's admira-tion inevitably perform prodigies of self-mortification. Father Donissan in *The Star of Satan* and Don Ardito Piccardi in both *The White Stone* and *Heaven and Earth (Il Cielo e la Terra)* whip them-selves mercilessly. The Curate of Ambricourt subsists on a diet of bread and wine. These priests are Romantic figures, not only because they are so clearly out of the past, but because they are thoroughly misunderstood and even victimized by Church and believer alike.

The best way for a non-believer to approach them is as Christian modulations of the solitary Romantic Chattertons whose lives re-enact the martyrdom of St. Sebastian. They endure the arrows of the world and often die beautiful young poetic deaths: young deaths though they be aged indeed, for they have remained children in spirit (and children still believe in chivalry and purity). Donissan is insti-tutionalized after carrying the body of the exorcized Mouchette to the church; Don Ardito Piccardi returns to his former parish as a vagrant and, ironically, receives a rich man's funeral to celebrate the Pharisaic Morosini's tenth anniversary as curate of Villanuova. The Curate of Ambricourt is "suspected of being a poet" by his Church superior. The priest is told the "truth" in no uncertain terms:

> The seminary is not the world, you know—real life is not like that. I don't think it would need much to turn you into an in-tellectual, that is to say, a rebel, systematically in revolt against every form of social superiority except those derived from the in-tellect.

Both Ambricourt and Don Ardito keep diaries, and the diary is, after all, a form of Romantic self-scrutiny, if it is not indeed Nar-cissism. As one unpleasant critic of Bernanos puts it, in a depressingly edifying book, *Guides vivants sur nos routes [Living Guides on our pathways]*, "our village priests, nowadays, have other things to do than transcribing their gastric troubles in diaries." It is revealing that both priests are avid readers of the *Imitation*, for their lives are moulded on that Medieval guide to the ascetic life. In an almost Pro-methean way, they become obsessed with the temptations of saint-hood. They strive, usually with nefarious results, to resuscitate the age of miracles. Ardito may have cured a case of paralysis; Donissan performs a rite of exorcism on the possessed Mouchette, leading to a possible conversion *in extremis,* but he also tries in vain to resurrect a dead child and in so doing drives its mother insane. The Church hierarchy is revolted by these goings-on (a reaction confirmed by Morris West's *The Shoes of the Fisherman* and Rolf Hochhuth's *The Deputy*); the Church is afraid of the supernatural, Ardito concludes ironically. The Church herself burned her greatest French saint, Péguy and Bernanos never tire of telling us. A similar pattern is discernible in the early writings of Julien Green. In his first pub-lished work, *Pamphlet against French Catholics,* he attacks the lukewarm, advocating a return to the Middle Ages or at least the Inquisition. In his journal, he tells us that while rereading the *Lives of the Desert Fathers*, he witnessed what was almost a rebirth of his adolescent feelings: "I thought I felt a glimmer of that supernatural fever which stirred the young Church. I wanted to gallop straight to Paradise."

What the novelists in question and their priest-heroes are ultimately exorcizing is the modern Church herself, the Church which, in their view, had become a faithful reflection of the general corruption of our times. The crucifix (in J. F. Powers' *Lions harts, leaping does*) is covered with lipstick after the veneration by the pious parish ladies. One of the Church officials whom Bernanos most clearly despises sings the praises of "that class of small, hardworking, thrifty shopkeepers, who are still the backbone and greatness of our dear France." The hatred of money and those contaminated by it is typical, of course, from Dostoevsky through Graham Greene, passing through Richard Wagner's Alberich, Drumont's attacks on *La France Juive*, Hillaire Belloc's *Emmanuel Burden*. Bernanos' priest-heroes, Donissan, Abbé Chevance and the Curate of Ambricourt, do more than live in utter poverty; they are from poor families and give away their possessions in extravagant acts of charity worthy of Dostoevsky. Donissan, characteristically, is first seen covered with dirt after working on a scaffolding with some builders. Bernanos' one priest villain is a rich intellectual, Abbé Cénabre. Another priest, likeable but unspiritual, admits that "the life I live here is in appearance that of a well-heeled layman." To give but one example of the attitude of an authentically poor priest, Don Ardito, in *Heaven and Earth* by Coccioli contemplates giving away his inheritance but has his doubts: "Don't the Scriptures say—'Woe unto you that are rich, for you have received your consolation'? I wondered whether we have any right to enrich our neighbor and thus cause him to lose his inheritance in heaven." The political implications of this attitude are enormous, for it is precisely this reasoning which leads a Bernanos and a Dostoevsky to despise socialism (it takes away the Christian poverty which makes the poor sacred unto God). Our writers' attitude toward the Church structure can best be summed up by citing a scene from the novel of a non-Christian writer who nonetheless relies on Christian symbolism. The one uncorrupted priest in *Bread and Wine (Pane e vino)* by Ignazio Silone dies while celebrating mass, because the sacramental wine had been poisoned. His name is Don Benedetto: the blessed are killed by the very substance of the now corrupt Church.

Our solitary Romantic priest-heroes are invariably overcome in their idealistic struggle to purify the Church. The poetic wand of analogy of the novelist conjures up a more radical exorcism. The Church herself must be persecuted or at least seek to leave its European institutions behind if she is to recover her primitive integrity. Querry, the church architect of *A Burnt-out Case*, has long since stopped building churches for religion; he builds them for Art: "Men have prayed in prison, men have prayed in slums and concentration camps. It's only the middle class who demand to pray in suitable surroundings," he remarks. Querry is one of Eliot's *Hollow Men* at the beginning of the novel; his trip up the Congo River into the heart of Africa reminds us of Eliot's epigraph from Conrad's *Heart of Darkness.* But Querry's sojourn in the leproserie turns out to be not an escape but a confrontation. The priests and even the atheistic doctor are not afraid of the biblical kiss to the leper. "It's a strange Christianity we have here," one of the priests tells Querry, "but I wonder whether the apostles would find it as difficult to recognize as the collected works of Thomas Aquinas." Despite the Pharisee Rycker's insistence that Querry is building a modern church, a "prayer in stone," Querry is building a primitive hospital, not a work of art. He is rejoining the tradition of the anonymous medieval churchbuilders whose buildings were useful not ornamental: "which one of us knows the architect of Chartres? He didn't care. He worked with love, not vanity,—without the trappings of civilization. (The Superior of the leproserie thinks that bidets are footbaths!) It is a world where the primitive Church has not yet been corrupted; where lost innocence has not yet been lost, as Greene says in his paean to Africa, *Journey without Maps.* All goes well in Querry's unsought-for rehabilitation, until, encouraged by Rycker, a journalist from a mass-circulation newspaper prints a story about the new African Saint-Querry.

> Historic Christianity has always believed in the valour of St. Michael riding in front of the Church militant, and in . . . the intoxication of the spirit, the wine of the blood of God.

These words by Chesterton are echoed by the whiskey priest in *The Power and the Glory*. He daydreams of Michael slaying the dragon. The whiskey-priest is the last priest in a godless totalitarian state, an outlaw in the eyes of the state, and in the eyes of the Church too because of his marriage. His religion is truly underground. Seen from the outside he is a renegade; seen from within, as a consecrated priest, he is the bearer of the sacraments. Querry returns to 'partial faith,' if this is indeed possible, through his encounter with the leper, Deo Gratias. The whiskey priest, in Dostoevskian fashion, finds at least a glimmer of redemption amidst the squalor of a common criminal's cell. He is a saint, as R. W. B. Lewis has pointed out (in *The Picaresque Saint*), precisely *because* he is persecuted. When priests were still respectable, he was decidedly lukewarm himself. In other words, it is *because* the Church has gone underground that the sacraments have been endowed with new vitality. Péguy's statement that the sinner is at the heart of Christianity, which served, by the way, as epigraph to *The Heart of the Matter* by Greene, is here revised to read: the sinner is at the very heart of sanctity. Greene provides his own gloss on the saga of the whiskey priest by interpolating at key moments the story of the martyr Juan, which a young Catholic mother is reading clandestinely to her children. That story is a direct parallel to the priest and the underground Church: Juan is a Mexican schoolboy who plays the part of Nero in a school play about the persecution of the early Christians. He becomes a priest and is executed by a revolutionary firing squad. His last words—'Viva el Cristo Rey!' It is in this family that the disguised successor to the executed whiskey priest will find refuge. The underground Church will continue, and as long as the Church is persecuted, she will remain pure, Greene intimates.

The post World War II renascence in German fiction is different from the *Konvertitenliteratur* (of Werfel and von Le Fort, say), of an earlier period. If one is German, one must obviously go through the Inferno before reaching the Paradiso (or the Purgatory of the *Wirtschaftswunder*). The problem of guilt, both national and personal, is all pervasive. As Sichelchen says in Langgässer's *The Quest*:

> "Humanity feels that it is approaching the hour when, in order to find salvation, it must be cast into the fire, into a fire of purgation of unparalleled intensity that nothing can extinguish. Listen to me, my friends, without fire salvation is impossible."

In a country where the Swastika has replaced the wooden cross of Jesus (the image is Böll's), the Romantic storybook symbol of the Christian Knight is patently an impossibility after World War II. The soldiers in the novels of Heinrich Böll, as we shall see later, are victims rather than makers of history. In *The Quest*, Elisabeth Langgässer's best novel, a group of pilgrims wander through the wasteland rubble of Germany, seeking salvation at the Convent of Anastasiendorf:

> Amid the fresh deposit of miserable old rubbish scarcely a speck of earth worthy of the name was anywhere discernible. Everywhere the ground was studded with glass and shells, and the place might just as well have been some landmark of Saturn, or a mountain pass on the moon . . . . It was turned inside out, this old earth, so plowed up that what still went by the name was something quite different—namely Tartarus.

The convent is in complete contrast to this landscape of Hell; there are no knights, but what the pilgrims and Langgässer see is more than a consecrated center of worship. Anastasiendorf is a symbol of a primitive agrarian civilization, self-sufficient and seemingly unaffected by the agony of Hitler's Germany. Böll's description of the Abbey of St. Anthony, in *Billiards at Half-past nine*, which I shall later examine in detail, looks back to a similarly idyllic past (as does his predilection for rural Ireland in the *Irish Diaries*).

The pattern is maintained as a concomitant of Catholic nostalgia for a medieval eden. Julien Green, upon hearing the news of the fall of France, begins to feel increasingly that he is indeed a Frenchman (which he is not!). In his *Memories of Happy Days*, he reminisces about his youth in France, recalling that although he was not yet a Catholic at the time, he was taken to mass in a fourteenth-century country church by some neighbors;

> Like the rest of the congregation she sang the Credo lustily, making the Latin words ring under the high Gothic vault much as they had done, century after century, in the very place where I stood. There was a strong appeal to my imagination in this thought. To be able to go back in time and in some curious way to find my place there, gave me a feeling of security which I am at a loss to explain and can only describe by saying that I delighted in fancying that I mingled with a medieval crowd. This perpetual harking back to the past, to a past which I had not known, was becoming part of my mental makeup . . . .

In other words, faced with the disorder of a defeated France, Green looks back to an orderly past, a Christian past, and, above all, an imaginary past. In Carlo Coccioli's *The Little Valley of God, (La Petite Vallée du Bon Dieu)*, the time of the threshing used to be a festive occasion, but now "a frigid silence reigned in the farmsteads." The hatred and suspicion last until a strange young man named Emmanuel appears and asks to join in the work. He begins to sing, and "this singing was a ray of sunlight that melted the ice in their hearts." The old times have returned. Emmanuel reminds us of Chesterton's Nicaraguan officer in *Napoleon of Notting Hill*. The new times lack festiveness despite the striving for gaiety.

> The fog lifts, the world sees us as we are, and worse still we see ourselves as we are. It was a carnival ball, my dear, which when the guests unmasked at midnight was found to be composed entirely of imposters. Such a *rumpus*, my dear.
>
> (Evelyn Waugh)

The burnt-out cases, the hollow-men, the imposters can only be exorcised by the magical return ot the beautiful, glowing times of which Novalis spoke. Those were times of prayer, not splenetic boredom, those were times of action, not paralysis:

> Some sneer, some snigger, some simper;
> In the youth where we laughed and sang,
> And *they* may end with a whimper,
> But *we* will end with a bang.
>
> (Chesterton)

Chapter II

The Supernatural in the Catholic Novel

The mirror in the road, as Stendhal well knew, is earthbound, and moving in human time and space, the novel cannot reflect Dante's vision of Beatrice as the living ray of Supreme Light. Our Catholic novelists would be only too willing to agree to this stricture. In his *Mémoires intérieurs*, François Mauriac confessed without reluctance that fiction, even when it does admit the active presence of Grace in the world, merely has the effect of cheapening a truth which is not the product of novelistic invention or transcription but necessarily beyond the power of words to communicate. Mauriac's famous definition of himself as "a metaphysician working concretely" is of necessity, and by authorial design, quoted in every critical study of his work. And for once Georges Bernanos would agree with the adversary he was later to deride as "less a man of good will than a man of good intentions." In an interview granted to Frédéric Lefèvre shortly after the publication of *The Star of Satan*, he stated that "The lived experience of divine love does not fall within the novel's province. But if I force the reader to descend to the depths of his own conscience, if I demonstrate to him, with persuasive evidence, that human weakness is not the final explanation, that this weakness is sustained and exploited by a ferocious and somber being, what choice does he have but to throw himself on his knees, if not with love then at least through fear, and to call God?" Despite Bernanos' rhetorical question, there *is* another alternative for the reader, especially if he is *extra muros* (Does a stained-glass window *exist* for those looking at it from *outside* the Church?) He will view evil as moral rather than metaphysical. He will disdainfully relegate Mauric's vision of female sexuality ("that shameful wound of nature, that cave of pestilence") to the category of sexual pathology; he will explain Bernanos' obsession with the devil's reality as vestigial Romantic satanism resulting from an overdose of Barbey d'Aurevilly; he will reject the spiritual validity of Bloy's (and Dostoevsky's) cult of regenerative suffering as just so much *Schadenfreude*. Small wonder, then, that from Porfiry in *Crime and Punishment* to *La Pérouse* in Bernanos' *La Joie* psychologizers and psychology itself are viewed as dangerously subversive, even heretical. The hypothetical extramural reader who (as defined above) is not too uncommon would deny the existence of "the Catholic novel."

The point is that the Mauriacs, Julien Greens and Joseph Malègues, their disclaimers notwithstanding, depend on the adumbration of the supernatural to give their works that metaphysical dimension which makes them "Catholic." In a beautiful analogy, Mauriac writes of the miracle at Cana: "the water was changed to wine, but there had to be natural water to make the wine precious." One might add that to understand the true symbolic nature of the water one needs the miracle of the wine. Would Mauriac's *The Desert of Love* be in any sense a religious novel if the heroine had not been named Maria Cross? Would Monsieur Ouine's aridity be anything more than psychological if the Curate of Fenouille had not, in his sermon, forced us to accept mental illness as a metaphor for demonic possession? Bernanos had proposed to show the reader evidence that human frailty is not the ultimate explanation for evil. This evidence, which is to force the reader to his knees, presupposes the supernatural, even if the novel's 19th century positivistic antecedents preclude the direct narration in prose of the kind of ecstasy Pascal sought to convey in the *Mémorial*. And if the Catholic novelists did not try to communicate the supernatural, many critics would have found their works less refractory.

My inquiry here will therefore seek to discover to what extent the need to communicate the supernatural somehow does in fact determine, influence or undermine the novelist's creation. Is he forced to invent new narrative devices, to modify traditional concepts of novelistic structure? Or is the Catholic novel simply a novel whose themes, preoccupations and values are determined by the author's "otherworld" view?

Since so many religious writers of all categories and persuasions insist on the inadequacy of words to communicate the workings of the supernatural, it should come as no surprise that our Catholic novelists strive to endow silence and absence with a positive function or value. Yet another trait they share with Romantics! They do this *by consciously structuring works that are formally complete to give the illusion of fragmentation.* It has, of course, become a virtual commonplace of post-Mallarméan criticism to affirm that the white spaces on the page can be meaningful, or in a different domain that the full-measure rests following the organ-like fanfares in Bruckner's symphonies are metaphors for the diffusion of prayerful echoes in Austrian baroque churches. The emotional climaxes of the sufferings of Goethe's Werther are often to be found in the missing letters, or, better, still, in those lines that have been rendered illegible by the correspondent's generous tears. The example of Dostoevsky is more directly relevant. His most rigidly structured novel, *Crime and Punishment,* ends with an epilogue, and the words:

> But that is the beginning of a new story, the story of the gradual rebirth of a man, the story of his gradual regeneration, of his gradual passing from one world to another, of his acquaintance with a new and hitherto unknown reality. That might be the subject of a new story—our present story is ended.

One notes the repetition of *gradual.* Surely the gradual transformation of a man is the very stuff of which novels are made. But this is transformation by Grace, "a new and hitherto unknown reality," and the novelist gives a very complete novel an illusion of incompletion. The novel ends by opening toward a silent future, and that vast blank is supposed to contain the supernatural. The conclusion of François Mauriac's *Evil (Le Mal)* is strikingly similar. The pious Fabien Dézaymeries succumbs to evil in the person of the femme fatale, Fanny Barrett; he tries clumsily to protect the malleable convent-girl, Colombe (!) from becoming another Fanny; and finally, thanks to the accusing presence of the non-believing Jewish student, Jacques Mainz (who views him as a representative of Catholicism), Fabien repentantly returns to the home of his Pharisee Mother half-dead from pneumonia:

That is why it would be suitable to begin here the true story of Fabien Dézaymeries, for which what has preceded could serve as prologue. But the totally internal drama of a man who covers his body with mud—a drama conveyed neither by words nor gestures—how to describe it? What artist would dare to imagine the movements and the ruses of Grace, that mysterious protagonist? It is our servitude and our misery (as artists) to be able to paint truthfully only those passions which are human.

When the apostate priest Cénabre, "that living being already dead," examines the body of the murdered Chantal de Clergerie—that "still living-though-dead being"—at the end of Bernanos' *Joy*, he asks the cook Fernande whether she can recite the Pater:

> "Say it once more," he said gently. "I can't."
> "Our Father, which art in Heaven," she began softly, with the inflection of the *Pays d'Auge*.
> "PATER NOSTER," said Cénabre with a superhuman voice.
> And he fell forward on his face.

A laconic and coldly objective footnote informs us that Abbé Cénabre died on March 10, 1912, "without having recovered his reason." We are inevitably driven to conjecture on the meaning of his madness: a metaphor for renewed faith with his reason representing his doubt? The novelist could have had Cénabre die on the spot, with the words of the Pater still on his lips. That would have been too clearcut. The footnote ensures that the reader will continue to speculate in perplexity on the meaning of Cénabre's last days and, hopefully, on the whole notion of Grace. But even if the novel *had* ended with Cénabre's death, Bernanos might have achieved a similar effect. For if a positivist views death as a completion, a fulfillment or definition of life, the Catholic novelist (there are fourteen narrated death agonies in the works of Bernanos alone) uses death to project his characters toward a silent, unknown future. There *is* life after death, not only in the effect a dead character produces on those who survive but also, and primarily, because death is a beginning, "the end of the night" (as Mauriac put it in the title of a sequel to *Thérese Desquéroux*); perhaps, too, the beginning of a *Vita Nuova*, one which the narrator consistently refuses to narrate. *Our story is completed* at death, but the Catholic novelist's tale becomes a fragment with the death of his central character.

II

It is within the body of the text itself that the 'illusory fragment' most radically affects novelistic technique. When the hero of Graham Greene's *The Heart of the Matter* slumps to the ground after a deliberate overdose of evipan, his dying sentence is broken by ellipses: "Dear God, I love . . . " We are never told whether Scobie's last word would have been "Louise" (his Pharisee wife), "Helen" (his mistress), "Ali" (the servant boy for whose death he feels responsible), or indeed "God." The journal of Mauriac's spiteful narrator, in *Vipers Tangle,* is interrupted by his death and by two lines of ellipses after the words: "this love of which I finally know the na . . . " The diary of Bernanos' country priest, while ending with a complete, even aphoristic, sentence necessarily breaks off before his death and final awareness of Grace. Throughout the novel, Bernanos had used italicized parentheses, numerous instances of pages torn out or missing, lines carefully erased, incomplete thoughts.

Each of these major Catholic novels might well have ended with ellipses. What happens instead is a direct consequence of the novelist's acknowledgement of *his* incapacity to deal honestly with the supernatural. *The narrative point of view changes;* we find a new narrative voice, one which is intentionally granted to *a flawed character completely unable to communicate or even to understand* the full dimensions of another's spiritual experience. Greene's *The Heart of the Matter* (of which more in Chapter VI) ends with three short dialogues appraising Scobie's death; dialogues between the treacherous Wilson and Louise, between his mistress Helen Rolt and her drunken wooer, Bagster, and finally between Louise and Father Rank. None of these characters had ever fully comprehended the religious struggle which preceded, and caused, Scobie's suicide. At best, Father Rank, the dead man's confessor, who should know the dark night of his parishioner's soul, proffers the inadequate summation: "It may seem an odd thing to say, when a man's as wrong as he was—but I think, from what I saw of him, that he really loved God." *Vipers Tangle* ends with two letters: from the venal Hubert to his sister Geneviève to express his horror at his father's

venomous diary, which he calls psychotic; and from Louis' grand-
daughter Janine to Hubert to protest his refusal to let her read the
diary despite her narration of Louis' apparent contrition: "an admir-
able light touched him during his last days." The reader, for reasons
I shall explore later, knows far more about the state of the narrator's
soul than either of these characters. Bernanos' Curate of Ambricourt's last moments are recounted in a letter from the defrocked
priest Dufréty to the Curate of Torcy. To the very end, Dufréty
retains his Dostoevskian defensive mask, and if, as he insists, he does
faithfully transcribe the country priest's final words "All is Grace,"
he is so paralyzed by his own psychic needs that he cannot grasp
the full significance of Grace as a reflection of the priest's death
agony.

Examples of this recourse to change in narrative point of view
to communicate the supernatural abound. There is May's occasional
religious diary in Mauriac's *Flesh and Blood (La Chair et le Sang),*
or Sarah Miles' journal in Greene's *The End of the Affair.* We hear of
Mouchette's so-called conversion *in articulo mortis,* in *The Star of
Satan,* when an obtuse and psychoanalytically oriented "Monseigneur" writes to a colleague. Father Donissan's ecstatic attempt to
resurrect a dead child is recounted in his own notes "written in haste,
and in a mental confusion approaching delirium. The wording is so
awkward and naive that it is impossible to transcribe these notes
without editing." We also read the official report submitted to the
Church authorities by the cautious and unspiritual Curate of
Luzarnes. The most vivid examples are to be found in Dostoevsky.
In *Crime and Punishment,* the reader has studied Raskolnikov's
spirit and psyche in monologues, repeated dream sequences, confrontations with confessors and doubles for more than 500 pages. Yet
when it comes to the epilogue and the first signs of spiritual illumination in Siberia, Dostoevsky makes it appear that the child-like
Sonya, one of his 'silent saints', has some responsibility for the
narration:

> At first Sonya's letters seemed rather dry and unsatisfactory to
> Dunya and Razumikhin, but in the end both of them found that the
> letters could not be better, as they conveyed a complete picture of

the life of their unhappy brother . . . . *Instead of attempting to describe Raskolnikov's state of mind and his thoughts and feelings generally, she gave them the mere facts* (itals. mine).

Again, it is the inefficient and inadequate narrator who by giving the "mere facts" suggests that the latent, mystical events were of such magnitude as to defy narration!

In *The Brothers Karamazov,* Father Zossima's exhortations are born in an ecstatic moment of illumination, and characteristically Dostoevsky disclaims responsibility for narrating them fully:

> The elder, however, spoke much more disjointedly than it is stated here or than Alyosha wrote down his words afterwards. Sometimes he broke off altogether, as though husbanding his strength, his breath failing him, but he seemed to be in a kind of ecstasy.

Zossima's confessions also move toward the fragmentary, since they are a narration of mystical conversion, the intervention of the supernatural within the novelistic fabric:

> Here I must note that this last conversation of the elder with his visitors on the last day of his life has been partially preserved in writing. It was written down from memory by Alexey Karamozov a short time after the elder's death. But whether it was all the conversation on that evening or whether he added to it from his notes of former talks with his teacher, I cannot say for certain? . . . Moreover, there can be no question of any uninterrupted narrative on the part of the elder, for sometimes he was gasping for breath, his voice failed him, and he even lay down to rest on his bed though he did not fall asleep and his visitors did not leave their seats.

What I am trying to show through these examples is that at critical times, when the supernatural becomes the very substance of the narrative, the author admits the infirmity of this omniscience and withdraws strategically, putting the responsibility for the narration on a witness *whose very inadequacy defines his function.* The reader hopefully infers that some essential is missing in the verbal texture, something beyond the power of words, and that "essence" is the supernatural. Mauriac gives us a good clue to this strategy in the preface to his *Three Tales (Trois Récits)*. By stressing the recurrence of certain themes and motifs (in that authorial assumption of divine omniscience that Sartre found so vexatious), he tries to demonstrate the implicit unity and Catholic potential of three separate stories; but his final words do not conclude—they open onto the implicit, the unstated: " 'To offer oneself to inspirations by humiliations.' The most beautiful story in this collection and which ought to bear inscribed this Pensée of Pascal is the fourth, the story the author did not write, that he was not yet worthy of writing."

This need to communicate Grace *through omission* modifies both the Catholic novelists' standards of plot design and characterization. The 19th century novel had trained us to hold an author accountable for the plausibility of his characters' actions. We are constantly asking "Why?" And if the explanation we are seeking is not psychological, we make do with environmental, hereditary, or (on a more sophisticated level of appreciation) structural justifications for plot movements and changes in character. Though Mauriac and Bernanos have both won admiration as perceptive psychologists, I think that one can safely state that when it comes to the salvation of a soul they do not hesitate to violate the prescriptions for motivation or preparation established by the novel's traditional positivism. Indeed, they often deliberately suppress plausible motivation since Grace is not for them psychologically analyzable. One important explanation for the presence of so many caricatural psychologists in Bernanos' novels is to show the reader how little a La Pérouse (the psychoanalyst in Bernanos' *Joy*) can understand the mystic, Chantal de Clergerie. One might, of course, criticize the many abrupt plot reversals and character transformations in Catholic novels as facile *deux ex machina scribendi*. Whether these peripeteia are successful or not novelistically is debatable; they are nonetheless elements in a purposeful literary strategy. Julien Green, Mauriac and Bernanos are not incapable of psychological verisimilitude: countless persuasive pages analyze the psychology of evil—Monsieur Ouine, Cénabre and Mauriac's Gabriel Gradère are fully portrayed and convincing while they are doing their evil deeds. But how can we justify Gradère's sudden metamorphosis, to cite but one of many examples.

We are at a loss to find within the text and within the character of Gradère adequate motivation or even foreshadowing for the words: "I am dying in peace . . . what indescribable peace." Yet this change takes place at the very end of the novel as Gradère lies dying, at the very moment of a Catholic novel when character development and plot are fused in death.

Further examples will help to focus the problem. In *The Star of Satan,* Mouchette cuts her throat with a razor after her meeting with Donissan. The priest had seen through her, had wrested the secret of the murder from her and by placing her crime into the context of generations of corruption, a "communion of sinners," had seemed somehow to absolve her of responsibility, to assume the burden of her sin himself. If Bernanos had *wanted* to explore the workings of Grace, he could have made Donissan's intervention so successful that Mouchette's self-destructive urge would have been broken. She would then not have killed herself, and the story of her regeneration might have made a good, though perhaps too edifying, Catholic novel. Instead, he lets her death agony last just long enough for her to express the final wish to be carried to the church to die. Many critics have offered thematic justification for this turn of events: the demon-haunted Donissan has made Mouchette aware of Satan while "depriving her of her crime" (her secret source of pride and her only reason for living); or the priest is himself tainted by satanism and unable to save souls, etc. But these explanations, while wholly consistent with Bernanosian thematics, do not explain why Donissan should be more effective at the dying girl's bedside than earlier. Nor do we directly witness Mouchette's conversion in extremis. We learn of her desire to die near the church in a new narrative, a letter from "Monseigneur" to Canon Gerbier. Once again, I think that one must conclude that Bernanos has deliberately chosen *not* to bear witness to this psychologically implausible reversal of character in order to suggest, through authorial abdication, the essential mystery of this transformation. This reluctance becomes all the more striking when we remember Bernanos' almost obsessive interest in narrated death agonies elsewhere.

III

How then can we measure the progress of salvation or damnation within a character? The narrator of *Vipers Tangle* is greeted by his family's recriminations when he returns home too late to say a final farewell to his wife Isa. Louis finds himself growing understandably sentimental, and when he discovers among the charred remains of Isa's papers some still decipherable words indicating that she had not reciprocated his hatred, his own heart of vipers is at least partially mollified. Louis' brief show of compassion for the disturbed Janine, his bursts of religiosity, even his visits to the Curate of Calèse can be psychologically accounted for—his deep-seeded hatred had resulted from his youthful jealousy of Isa's tears for her former suitor Rodolphe; his repressed thirst for affection now surges to the surface, and so on. But the illumination by Grace hinted at by the final lines of his diary cannot be seen as consistent with his character, although Hubert diagnoses: "evidence of intermittent delirium," urging that the diary be submitted as a case study to a psychiatrist. There is nothing inherent in Louis' character, nothing at least as the novelist has had him present it to the reader of his journal, to prepare the final epiphany.

Yet if we do not relegate Louis' transformation to the category of psychological disturbance, it is because Mauriac has taken precautions to insure that this conversion is accepted at full spiritual value. Unwilling to make manifest the continuing presence of redemptive forces *within* Louis' soul, the author has created a series of secondary characters whose *principal function is to embody in a form external to the hero the inner world of the tormented Louis.* These characters are to be echoes or shadows of deeper spiritual strains of innocence that would otherwise be unexpressed. Each of these "doubles" is a child or essentially childlike, each of them is instinctively drawn to Louis despite his apparent misanthropy. And because they are childlike, the author is freed of the task of endowing each of them with a complex autonomous personality containing its own contradictions, an obligation which might have compromised their role as doubles.

Mauriac structures the lines of his plot to permit the sequential introduction of these characters. There is Louis' daughter Marie, the only one of his children to have loved him and for whose death Isa tries to make him feel responsible. The others are in a way replacements for Marie. There is Abbé Hardouin: "he took my hand and said to me those unbelievable words which I heard for the first time in my life and which put me in a kind of stupor: 'You are very good.' " There is Marinette's son Luc ("he was nature itself"), who becomes Marie's "brother" in the narrator's eyes and who sends him a card from the Front where a figurative conventional formula "Tendresses" (Tenderly) takes on a sudden literal meaning. These characters become fused in the person of his great-grand-daughter, the consolation of Louis' last days:

> It was in my arms, on my knees, that the little girl sought refuge while waiting for dinner to be served. In her hair, I found the smell of young birds in their nest which reminded me of Marie . . . . It was also, and at the same time, Luc I thought I was kissing.

And there is Janine, who in her anguish has become the reincarnation of Marinette and the witness of her grandfather's final delirious confusion: "Grandfather is the only religious man whom I have ever met," she says to Hubert; this about the man who was a self-proclaimed atheist and anti-clerical!

Georges Bernanos makes even more effective use of the double as a substitute for necessarily inadequate novelistic psychology. If Cénabre (in *L'Imposture /Imposture/*), upon hearing the satanic laughter celebrate his loss of faith, turns toward his mirror only to see there "the intolerable reflection of a face transformed by fear, of a miserable body in full flight," his summoning of the childlike Abbé Chevance, his opposite and yet also the embodiment of a residue of innocence within him which will lead to his possible reconversion later, marks a confrontation with another aspect of his own soul. In *Diary of a Country Priest*, the Countess's innocence is represented by the curate himself. His long conversation with her, culminating in his symbolic gesture of reaching into the flames to pull out the locket which she tried to burn because it contained a picture of her dead son), represents the externalization of a struggle that is taking place within the Countess's soul at the precise moment when her demonic hatred fuses with his willingness to risk the flames of hell for her soul.

The doctrine of Substitution or vicarious suffering has often
been adduced in analyzing the problem of the double in Catholic
novels. Gabriel Gradère's sudden reversal of character, unexplained
and unmotivated, deprives his double, the priest Alain Forcas, of *his*
peace in Mauriac's *Dark Angels (Les Anges noirs)*. Bernanos' priests
constantly offer themselves as scapegoats. I cannot help but feel,
however, that Substitution, revealing as it is, does not satisfactorily
explain those scenes where there is no "exchange." Nor does it
account for the fact that so many Catholic novels are designed less
as a series of actions than of confrontations. When (Dostoevsky is
once more the prototype!) the story of Raskolnikov shifts from such
external events as the murder itself to the internal struggle between
good and evil within his soul, Dostoevsky largely eliminates the
dream sequences and soliloquies which dominated the first half of
Crime and Punishment and guides his hero to a series of meetings
with Svidrigailov and Sonya Marmeladov, the externalizations of
the satanic and divine elements of Raskolnikov's soul.

Not all novelistic devices resulting from the need to suggest
that the supernatural alone is responsible for psychologically unexplained reversals of character or plot are as successful. "The answered
prayer," for example, can be distinctly irritating: at a crucial moment of tension, a character utters a prayer. Many pages later, after
his life has taken an inexplicable direction completely inconsistent
with what has come before, the character comes to the realization
that this transformation had been due to the prayer's being granted.
Donissan's life of struggle against despair can be said to begin with a
prayer directed at the impassive Christ on the crucifix, but also at
Satan: "What have I left to give?, What have I left? Hope alone. Take
it from me. Take that too!" For Graham Greene's Sarah Miles, an
answered prayer marks both *The End of the Affair* and the beginning
of belief. During a bombing-raid on London, she had prayed for the
safety of her lover Bendrix:

> Dear God, I said—why dear, why dead? make me believe. I can't
> believe. Make me . . . . Let him be alive, and I *will* believe. Give him
> a chance . . . . I love him, and I'll do anything if You'll make him
> alive. I said very slowly, I'll give him up forever, only let him be
> alive with a chance.

Bendrix finds this prayer recorded in Sarah's journal. Now he can understand why she left him shortly after that terrifying night; and this awareness of the *answered paryer* as the key motivation for Sarah's subsequent faith leads the skeptical novelist himself toward some hesitant initial gropings toward belief: "I found the one prayer that seemed to serve the winter mood: O God, You've done enough, You've robbed me of enough. I'm too tired and old to learn to love. Leave me alone forever." The very act of addressing God is, of course, the gesture of prayer. And examples of answered prayers abound in Catholic novels.

The second questionable device, one I shall have occasion to find less questionable in my discussion of Flannery O'Connor's *Wise Blood* and *The Violent Bear it Away*, is the efficacy of sacrament. Elisabeth Langgässer has made the mysterious effects of baptism on an apparent non-believer the subject of her vast panoramic novel *The Indelible Seal*. In Mauriac's *That Which Was Lost*, Alain is at a loss to understand why he had long felt "different, as though shunted aside. What was this fate?" The reader is equally perplexed. It is only after having learned that his mother had had him secretly baptized to spite his free-thinking father that Alain can understand the mysterious vocatus which had governed his life (and the plot of the novel):

> It was gently sweet for him to know that he belonged to Christ. Was it the first time that Alain spoke this name aloud? To his very last breath, he would remember the thunder of that lone syllable sounding in the old bumpy omnibus on a route near Entre-deux-Mers one evening.

(The symbolic pun on *Mers /Mères/*, the sacred and profane mothers, measures Alain's spiritual state.) Similarly it is at Sarah Miles' funeral that Bendrix learns from her mother that she had been baptized a Catholic: "I always had a wish that it would *take*. Like vaccination." Bendrix refuses to believe that the first sacrament had *taken:* "You can't mark a two-year-old child for life with a bit of water and a prayer. If I began to believe that, I could believe in the body and the blood." But this is precisely what had happened. And the efficacy of the sacrament of ordination makes the ability of certain priest-figures to read in the souls of sinners a manifestation of the supernatural rather than a mere novelistic trick. Alyosha Karamazov "knows" that Ivan has been visited by the Devil. The Curate of Ambricourt "knows", in a flash of illumination, that Chantal's purse contains a letter of despair, just as Chesterton's Father Brown often catches the criminal by sensing the presence of Satan in a guilty soul. In this range of novelistic devices, the need for suspension of disbelief on the part of the reader, willing or unwilling, is obviously most acute.

IV

    I have deliberately left to the last what may be the most interesting, as well as the most complex, technical problem posed by the supernatural. Novelists write fiction; Catholic novelists write fiction depending on a higher truth which, they believe, is not the product of man's invention, but of God's creation. God's universe, that of the Church, is allegorical: every gesture, every action, every object has a known value in a totally meaningful, all encompassing design. Dante could write of such a universe not only because he believed in it but because the Divine Comedy is situated in a realm of the mind. Even the most theocentric of 13th century Florentines could not claim to have empirical knowledge of the Inferno, Purgatorio or Paradiso, and with the exception of the poet himself all of the characters of the Comedy are dead. The novelist, as opposed to the allegorical poet, has his base in reality, at least if we accept Mauriac's emphasis on the concrete and Bernanos' affirmation that the "lived experience of divine love does not belong in the novel." Yet the novelist is constantly tempted by allegory in his tacit evocation of the supernatural, this in a deallegorized world of non-believers and of meaningless things. Kafka realized this; and so did Camus, when in *The Fall (La Chute)* he playfully introduces a swarm of consecrated religious symbols ranging from the title to a flight of doves. In a middle-class hell of a world whose order is ambiguous, these are non-symbols. Only on the football field, where there are still rules of the game, is allegory possible: the movement of the game itself is that of the traditional allegorical pilgrimage toward a goal: *un but*. The Catholic novelist still believes in the rules of the game, in a coherent system of meaningful symbols. He is constantly tempted by them to make the supernatural manifest: the novel would then become a vehicle for theological exegesis, not for literary criticism, since these symbols would not be organic to the particular novel under study. A traditional or consecrated allegory is a memory of a divinely ordered world. Every household in France, for example, receives the Post Office calendar of feast-days, which means that simply mentioning a date in a Catholic novel might set into motion a host of symbolic associations. Christening a character Sebastian, Theresa, Gabriel or Lazarus might thus determine his function and place in a universe ordered on other than novelistic principles. Bernanos must have been aware of this danger when he invented such names as Mouchette (baptized Germaine!), Donissan, Cénabre, Chevance; to foil the symbol-hunters even further he obstinately refused to give his priest heroes christian names, preferring at times to make them anonymous extensions of their parish: Curate of Ambricourt, etc. His awareness of the dangers of onomastics can be seen in the resonance uniting the Curate of Torcy's name, Martin, to that of his adversary, Luther. But the interpreters will not desist; they link Mouchette to the "candle-snuffer"; Donissan to *don au sang*, gift to blood, etc. What I am saying here is that it would be all too easy to create a network of recondite religious symbols which draw on the Church's symbolic view of the universe, whereas it is extremely difficult to use consecrated symbolism in such a way that it seems to grow out of the very substance of the novel.

François Mauriac is guilty of some flagrant lapses of novelistic taste, especially in works written after Jacques Maritain's famous criticism of his insufficiently aggressive Christianity. The title of *The Lamb (L'Agneau)* might have been sufficiently suggestive, as in *A Kiss to the Leper (Le Baiser au Lépreux)* or *The Dark Angels (Les Anges noirs)*. But the preachy post-Nobel Prize Mauriac of 1954 needed to affirm, to prove, not merely to adumbrate the supernatural. When Jean de Mirbel locks the little orphan Roland (!) in a room to punish him, the ex-seminarian Xavier (who had given up his theological studies to save Mirbel's marriage) takes a ladder to climb through the window of the locked room to watch over

Roland. The action itself would prove Xavier's compassion for suffering children and, coupled with the resonances of the novel's title, would indicate his Christ-like qualities. But Mauriac insists on belaboring the symbol. Roland, according to Xavier, is "one of those children that you and I must end up resembling." The ladder explicitly becomes the Cross when Xavier carries it on his shoulders, struggling to master the pain emanating from the stigmata-like wounds in his feet; and his tears of pain are "a tear, a drop of sweat or of blood."

It is a rare Catholic novelist who can avoid obvious symbolism by integrating traditional imagery into his work without forcing his characters into neat patterns. Mauriac succeeds at two points in *Vipers Tangle,* though, as we have seen, he often fails. When Louis returns home after Isa's death, he rummages about in her burned papers and finds that she feared for his salvation, that she loved him in the highest sense. Intent on further testimony, he probes deeper in the fireplace but without results. As he gets up, looking at his dirty hands, he turns toward the mirror: "I saw in the mirror my forehead scarred with ashes." The entire novel has led to this moment of contrition. "A desire to walk possessed me as in my youth." The ashes mark the beginning of Lent in Louis' soul, leading to the resurrection at the end of this diary. The ashes are the memory of the Palm Sunday of his youth, but also embody the life and death of Isa. And the suggestive word "scarred" *(balafré)* likens his life of torment to a wound. No priest is present to daub Louis' forehead with the ashes, but one feels that this complex symbol indicates a momentary intervention of the supernatural. This key scene had been foreshadowed by a moment of paternal communion with Luc, who was about to leave for the war. Louis' ultimate gesture of love had been to part with some of his angrily acquired gold, and he decided to make this offering to "my poor child." As he gets some gold out of the plaster head of Demosthenes (a lapse in taste, this: the mouth filled with pebbles or the name of his teacher Iseus— linked to Louis' wife Isa?), Louis rummages to find his money belt hidden there, and "that boa swollen and gorged with metal rolled itself around my neck, crushing my throat." The effect, despite the allegorical blunder of Demosthenes' name, is deeply suggestive of symbolism organically derived from the materials of the novel: boa reminds us of the fur which Luc's mother Marinette had worn on the day Louis had wiped her eyes with his handkerchief; it also stands for the real serpentine presence of Satan in Louis' lust for money, the avarice which had strangled his love, turning his family and his heart into a "Tangle of Vipers." But that very feeling of strangulation is that of a victim of a boa constrictor, "nourishing itself by crushing warm-blooded vertebrae with his powerful muscular grip," to quote a convenient dictionary. Mauriac denies himself the facile possibilities of a network of contrived religious associations with apple trees in the Garden of Eden.

It is at such moments, when the threads of realism and symbolism are naturally and inextricably intertwined, that the supernatural becomes, albeit briefly, legitimized within the novel. Such moments, fortunately, are rare. The reader feels far more comfortable with the shadow He casts than in encounters with the Light itself.

Chapter III

Perspectives on Georges Bernanos

A. Sous le Soleil de Satan: *The Prologue*

"I really think that my book is one of the books born out of the war," Georges Bernanos admitted in 1926 to the interviewer who had praised *The Star of Satan* as "the most beautiful war novel." Bernanos began his first novel shortly after the Armistice. The face of the world which until then had been only terrifying had now become hideous: "Universal *détente* was an unbearable spectacle." For Bernanos, who had been released from military service for medical reasons in 1911, only to reenlist at his own stubborn insistence in 1914, the long months in the front-line trenches had already provided a first experience of Hell. The rows of bayonets, the barbed-wire barriers, the relentless fog and rain, the mud everywhere: these are recurring motifs in Bernanos' war letters (and will furnish imagery to his novels). Nor did he forget that on the home front (*l'Arrière*, which he soon began to call *le Derrière*) the politicians and financiers were making their profitable deals. Above all, there was the gradual, tragic realization that the age of heroism was over, that here in the mechanized boredom of a war of waiting, the sense of risk and honor of the "poor horseman who only had his cape and sword" was a pitiful anachronism. Whatever Bernanos was to write subsequently, be it the novels or the polemic works, he remained faithful to the basic themes of his war letters to his fiancée and to his confessor Dom Besse: the obsessive hatred of money ("the blood of the poor," Bernanos' literary mentor Bloy called it) and of all associated with the world of finance (Jews in particular, as Drumont would have it); the nostalgia for an age of chivalry, the vision of mud

and boredom as the very staples of Hell. But it was life in the carnival atmosphere of post-Armistice Paris which proved an even more
shattering Inferno: "Whoever did not live through those times can
not know what disgust is all about," he wrote many years later. Disillusionment thrust me into literature," he was to explain. And elsewhere: "I did not want to die without bearing witness."

And yet in *The Star of Satan,* Bernanos' testimony seems
strangely abstract. Nowhere in the novel does the reader find a convincing and direct evocation of the specific events and conditions
which had allegedly irritated the author into writing. At least part
of the explanation lies in the resonances and overtones of the title
of the novel. *Sous le Soleil de Satan,* already diabolical in the serpentine hiss of its alliteration, should be translated "On Satan's
earth," for *sous le soleil* simply means on earth, and the earth, in
Bernanos' novels, is Satan's possession' "the prince of this world,"
he usually called him. The daring title revitalizes the common biblical expression "under the sun" by exploiting the allusion to *Eccle-
siastes:* "There is no new thing under the sun." Particular events
always fall into an eternally recurring pattern, and Father Donissan
can tell the murderess Mouchette that her life repeats other lives. By
deliberately avoiding a specific historical context in the most successful portions of this uneven novel, Bernanos generalizes the import of
his first book. Its temporal and spatial dimensions are spiritual and
internal rather than realistic or topical; the novelist is painting a symbolic tableau of Satan's reign in the modern world. I have already
quoted in full his remark to Lefèvre that by showing the reader that
human weakness does not of itself cause evil but that there is a
ferocious and somber spirit exploiting human frailty he would force
the reader to his knees. Perhaps it is this didactic motivation which
forces Bernanos to forsake, at least partially, the symphonic unity
of form dear to most French novelists of that time, creating in its
stead a kind of triptych with each panel focusing on a different
aspect of the Satanic presence: the physical with Mouchette, the
religious with Donissan, the intellectual with the novelist Antoine
Saint-Marin. The latter two receive treatment in this book in Chapter II
and in section B of this chapter. The first, "Histoire de Mouchette,"
is in many ways the most challenging, though because of its apparent
lack of obvious religious relevance it has often been summarily

dismissed as a skillful imitation of Barbey d'Aurevilly's short stories. In the triptych, Mouchette, Donissan and Saint-Marin are all three engaged in an novitiate in the cloisters of hell. Together, their story is Bernanos' allegory of the sensual, spiritual and intellectual predicaments of modern man.

"Histoire de Mouchette," which Bernanos calls the prologue to the novel proper, is almost embarrassingly uninventive if we consider the basic plot outline alone. The parents of Germaine Malorthy ("Mouchette" to her lovers) discover that she is pregnant. Hoping to strike an advantageous bargain, M. Malorthy goes to accuse the prime suspect, the Marquis de Cadignan, but after an argument succeeds only in being asked to leave. He orders his daughter to consult Dr. Gallet, who, in his double wisdom as man of science and member of Parliament, might offer a solution to the family's predicament. Germaine's categorical refusal results in her banishment from the Malorthy's comfortable brick house, but since the thought of escape had been seething within her anyway, she views her exile as a new found freedom. She runs straight to the château of the Marquis, where she begs him as the father of her unborn child to take her away to Paris, anywhere . . . The impecunious Cadignan finds only the most venal reasons for rejecting Mouchette's romantic scheme. In a fit of frustration and rage she takes down his gun and shoots him. All her dreams of liberation from the conventionality and materialism of her family are irrevocably compromised by the crime. Ironically, she is forced to return under the paternal roof in order to avoid becoming a suspect in the murder case. She succeeds completely, for the shot was fired from such a close angle that the death of the Marquis passes as a suicide. Now in a deliberate gesture of self-debasement she becomes the mistress of Dr. Gallet. The final scene of "Histoire de Mouchette" depicts her in a desperation verging on hysteria, vainly beseeching the doctor to perform an abortion, then trying to bind him to her forever by confessing the murder to him as though to a priest. Gallet, sensing that his public career might be in jeopardy, pretends not to believe her. Once again Mouchette's dreams have been frustrated. This time her escape is into madness. A laconic final paragraph informs us that a month later she was released from an asylum after her baby had been still-born. In the next section of the novel, "The Temptation of Despair," she will commit suicide by slashing her throat with her father's razor.

A melodramatic plot if ever there was one. The story of Mouchette might have tempted not only Barbey but a popular novelist of the milieu like Carco. It is the classic case history of the "fallen woman" of the time, as a sampling of faits-divers in any French provincial newspaper would quickly show: the deserted pregnant girl banished by her father and forced into prostitution, crime or suicide. There are situations in "Histoire de Mouchette" which are equally conventional, in fact seem to come straight from the boulevard theater: the lustful Marquis chasing his mistress around the table; the doctor hearing his wife's footsteps and trying to make his scene with the half-naked Mouchette look like a medical consultation. Yet strangely, the reader does not feel embarrassed by these details. Indeed, the very banality of the plot endows it with an uncanny allegorical power as the story of *a* Mouchette, one of thousands in France. "There is nothing new under the sun," the title of the novel reminded us. Recognizing an old story, the reader is forced to admit that melodrama is the stuff of reality; he can consequently direct his complete attention to the details of Bernanos' novelistic art which make the story transcend the vulgarity of the plot. Only at rare moments was Bernanos able to equal the disciplined cohesion and textual density of "Histoire de Mouchette."

The whole of *Sous le Soleil de Satan* seems to grow directly out of the arresting opening paragraphs, a poetic evocation of the coming of night:

> Voici l'heure de soir qu'aima P.-J. Toulet. Voici l'horizon qui se défait—un grand nuage d'ivoire au couchant et, du zénith au sol, le ciel crépusculaire, la solitude immense, déjà glacée—plein d'un silence liquide . . . Voici l'heure du poète qui distillait la vie dans son coeur, pour en extraire l'essence secrète, embaumée, empoisonnée.
>
> Déjà la troupe humaine remue dans l'ombre, aux mille bras, aux mille bouches; déjà le boulevard déferle et resplendit . . . Et lui, accoudé à la table de marbre, regardait monter la nuit, comme un lis.

> Here is the moment of evening which P. -J. Toulet loved. Here is the moment when the horizon undoes itself—a great ivory cloud in the sunset, and from the zenith to the earth, the sky of dusk, the immense, already chilled, solitude, all full of liquid silence . . . Here

is the moment for the poet who distilled life in his heart to extract
its secret essence, embalmed, envenomed.

Already the thousand-armed and thousand-mouthed human herd
stirs in the shadows; already the boulevards unfurl and glitter . . .
And he, leaning on his elbows on the marble-topped table, watches
the night rising, like a lily.

The reader is immediately alerted to the basically poetic texture of
what is to follow. Certain key words which will dominate the imagery
of the novel are stressed from the very beginning: *Solitude, silence,*
envenomed or poisoned *(empoisonnée)*, chilled or frozen *(glacée)*.
"What must I fear beside solitude and boredom?" Mouchette asks
herself before running away from home. In her womb and spirit
corruption blooms "like a fine flower full of venom." In the novel's
second section, "The Temptation of Despair," Donissan's encounter
with Satan takes place on a cold, rainy November night, and his
adversary admits: "I am cold itself" *(Je suis le Froid lui-même)*. The
twilight hour, the world of light, of the real sun, is in decomposition;
the reign of Satan's black sun ("the star denied by morning: Lucifer
or the false Dawn") begins. Most of the key scenes in the novel will
take place in darkness. Night for the escaping Mouchette opens
"like a sanctuary". As Donissan plods aimlessly across the plain
toward Satan's embrace, "the shadows were so thick that as far as
his glance could carry he could discover no brightness, not even
a reflection, none of those visible tremblings that are, even in the
deepest night, like the radiation of the living earth, the slow decomposition until day returns of the destroyed, previous day." The
final section of the novel, "The Saint of Lumbres," opens with
Donissan looking out of his window: "Across the abyss of shadow
glistening with rain, the church weakly shone, the only living being . . ."

The repeated *already (déjà)*, so prominently placed at the
beginning of the second paragraph, indicates Bernanos' despair at
the rapidity with which the artificial light of the boulevards has replaced the light of day. The horizon has decayed; the boulevard un-
furls like a triumphal banner and flows like a new sun. Though this
novel is set entirely in the countryside and villages of Bernanos'
Artois, he cannot resist evoking the man-swarm in the streets of the
city at night, perhaps because of his violent revulsion when faced
with the post-war merry-making of the Parisians. ("The temperature,

even under the February rain, was that of a brothel," he wrote else-where.) One might conclude, especially since so many of Bernanos' novels were composed while the novelist was seated at café tables, that the poet is the author himself, or perhaps Toulet. But, above all, he is Baudelaire. For the poet of the *Flowers of Evil (Les Fleurs du Mal)*, more than any other, extracted from life's distilled essence, something secret, embalmed and poisonous: the words themselves count among his favorites, which is why Bernanos uses them here. Moreover, the entire opening passage of *Sous le Soleil de Satan* was probably directly inspired by Baudelaire's *Recueillement (Meditation)* and *Le Crépuscule du soir (Evening twilight):*

> Sois sage, ô ma douleur, et tiens-toi plus tranquille.
> Tu réclamais le Soir; il descend; le voici.
> . . . .
> Pendant que des mortels la multitude vile,
> Sous le fouet du Plaisir, ce bourreau sans merci,
> Va cueillir des remords dans la fête servile,
> Ma Douleur, donne-moi la main; viens par ici . . .

> Be good, my sorrow, and keep still.
> You asked for evening, it's descending now, here it is.
> While the base crowd of mortals, under the whip of pleasure,
>   that merciless hangman,
> Gathers remorse in servile feasting,
> My sorrow, give me your hand; come here . . .
>   *(Recueillement)*

Bernanos chose Baudelaire to open his first novel because both share a common obsession with the reality of evil. Father Menou-Segrais echoes the poet's famous *double postulation* when he explains to Donissan: "Each of us is in turn a criminal or a saint, at times drawn toward good . . . at others tormented by a mysterious taste for self-debasement." Both writers see evil as tentacular. Late in the novel, Bernanos will develop his initial metaphor when he likens sin to "the horrible fibers of cancer, and its links retracting, like the detached arms of an octopus." And so the poet and the novelist together watch the night rise, like a lily. The simile, at first glance decorative, achieves its full ironic power only when we realize that the lily is the flower of purity, the symbol of the Virgin.

That Bernanos should have mentioned Toulet rather than Baudelaire in the crucial opening sentence of the novel is indeed surprising. The playfully ironic works of the author of *Les Contrerimes* could hardly inspire the fraternal sympathy of the visionary Catholic. Bernanos himself offers unsatisfactory explanations elsewhere, when he avers that he himself is intimidated by the first step in opening a novel and needs a protector (this in the preface to *Les Grands Cimetières sous la Lune [The Great Cemeteries in the Moonlight]*) or in more detail in his lecture "Satan and us":

> I still see myself, one September evening, the window opening onto a twilight sky. I thought of the ingenious P. -J. Toulet, of his green maiden, of his charming poems, sometimes winged, sometimes limping, full of secret bitterness. Then that little Mouchette surged forth . . . I saw that mysterious girl between her brewer-father and her mother. And bit by bit I imagined her story.

There is, to be sure, some resemblance between the youthful freshness of Sabine de Charité ("Guiche"), the heroine of Toulet's *La Jeune fille verte* (1920), and the graceful animality of Mouchette. Bur a more plausible reason for the prominence given to Toulet's name in Bernanos' opening sentence lies in the frivolous religiosity which dominates Toulet's novel. "Can love ever be demonic?" one of the many adulterous characters asks naively. In the shadows of the village church, Mme Beaudésyme finds only a fleshly mysticism whose *animal ecstasy* is perfectly sustained by the organ music, the incense, the echoes from the musty stones. When, at long last, a serious priest, Father Nicolle, arrives and agrees to hear confessions, his unindulgent rigor becomes all the rage among the fashionable ladies ("It's so much fun confessing, to tell *them* things".). Bernanos' Father Donissan is similarly a priest of the confessional during his tenure at Lumbres; he too will be misunderstood by the Pharisees. Toulet's novel may well have *provoked* Bernanos into writing, and it might well be his reaction against the religiosity of Toulet's characters, symptomatic as it is of the Pharisaism of the *bien-pensant* public, which accounts for the very limited importance of ritual in *Sous le Soleil de Satan.*

After the reflective lyricism of the opening night-scene, the tone changes abruptly when Bernanos tries to provide the social background for his story. The fact that the second paragraph begins with the same words as the first *(Voici l'heure . . .)* only accentuates the shock. This change marks, I think, one of those deplorable lapses of taste that occur all too frequently when Bernanos attempts expositions. His convictions are so strong that the satiric pamphleteer pushes the novelist aside to proffer a few journalistic *bons mots*. Thus, the Malorthy family heritage of liberalism leads to the comment: "The spiritual heirs of Blanqui people the register, and those of Lamennais encumber the sacristies." Gallet is a health-officer "nourished on the doctrines of Raspail," and the Marquis de Cadignan kept posted on world events by reading "the gossip column of *Le Gaulois* and the political reports of the Revue des Deux Mondes." Despite its flaws, this second introductory section has an important function. Bernanos is not interested in a detailed Balzacian setting for his story (though the name Cadignan is taken from Balzac). With a few brushstrokes he makes us feel that the town of Campagne is a microcosm of a spiritually and socially decadent France. The neutrality of the town's name further generalizes the import of the story. With the exception of Mouchette herself, the characters are clearly representatives, not individuals. There is the rising materialist Malorthy who had never asked for anything but an "honest profit." The power in the village is shared by two rivals: Dr. Gallet who stands for science and parliamentary democracy, and the useless aristocrat Cadignan, whose great passion is to rehabilitate the forgotten sport of hawking. In short, all of the things that Bernanos despises in modern France are present. Only the church and the priest are missing in this world of substitute religions. "A doctor stands for learning and science, he's not just a man, he's the parish priest of the republican," Malorthy explains (in a direct quotation from Barbey's story "Le bonheur dans le crime").

Now the story itself can begin. It is told with an economy of expression and a tightness of structure rare in Bernanos' work. A rapid series of dramatic confrontations in dialogue form (between Malorthy and Cadignan, Malorthy and Mouchette, Mouchette and Cadignan, and finally Mouchette and Dr. Gallet) is interrupted only by occasional semi-poetic comments on the inner turmoil of the heroine by an omniscient (and affectionate) narrator. There is a profound thematic justification for this arrangement. The entire fabric of human relationships has been eroded by mendacity. Malorthy lies to the Marquis, pretending that his daughter had already revealed the identity of her lover; he lies to Mouchette by accusing the Marquis of striking him. Mouchette replies that the Marquis had never touched her, which calls forth another lie by the father who swears that Cadignan has already confessed. The girl weaves a complicated tissue of lies in her interview with the Marquis. First, she pretends not to be pregnant; then she tries to make him jealous by referring to the romantic propositions of his arch-rival, Dr. Gallet; finally, she compounds the fiction when she announces that she is in fact already the doctor's mistress. In the final dialogue, she attempts to engage Gallet's responsibility by insinuating that he, not the Marquis, is the father of her child. Tragically, *the one time she tells the truth,* when she confesses the murder to Gallet, he pretends not to believe her. Bernanos himself quoted a revealing passage from Barbey's *Les Diaboliques* in a projected preface to his second novel, *L'Imposture;* "I am convinced that for certain souls there is joy in imposture."

Because of the breakdown of meaningful verbal communication in the dialogues, the novelist concludes that he alone can tell "the truth" about Mouchette and endow her with sufficient psychological (or spiritual) complexity. He frequently interposes his own comments by changing the *tone* of his narration from the detached stage directions which complement the dialogues to a more lyrical inflection, a peculiar blend of imagery and conceptual analysis:

> Elle essaya de secouer la tête d'un air de bravade; mais encore mal aguerrie, l'ignoble injure, frappée de près, la fit un instant plier: elle sanglota.
> —Tu en entendras bien d'autres, si tu vis longtemps, continua paisiblement le marquis. La maîtresse de Gallet! . . . A la barbe du papa, sans doute?
> —A Paris, quand je voudrai, bégaya-t-elle à travers ses larmes . . . oui! à Paris.

> Les dix petites griffes grinçaient sur la table, où elle appuyait ses mains. La rumeur des idées dans sa cervelle l'étourdissait; mille

mensonges; une infinité de mensonges y bourdonnaient comme une rûche. Les projets les plus divers, tous bizarres, aussitôt dissipés que formés, y déroulaient leur chaîne interminable, comme dans la succession d'un rêve. De l'activité de tous les sens jaillissait une confiance inexprimable, pareille à une effusion de la vie. Une minute, les limites mêmes du temps et de l'espace parurent s'abaisser devant elle, et les aiguilles de l'horloge coururent aussi vite que sa jeune audace . . .
-A Paris? dit Cadignan.

She tried to bluster, tossing her head, but she wasn't tough enough. For a second she waivered under the vile insult deeply thrust: she sobbed.
—You'll be hearing far worse if you live long enough, the marquis continued calmly. Gallet's mistress. Right in Papa's face, I bet?
—In Paris, whenever I want! she stuttered through her tears. "Yes, Paris."

Ten little claws scraped the table where she leaned her hands. The drone of ideas in her brain made her dizzy: a thousand lies; an infinity of lies buzzed as if in a hive. The wildest plans no sooner formed than dispersed unfolded their endless chain, as though in a dream-sequence. From the stirring of her senses surged an ineffable confidence, like an effusion of life. For an instant the very limits of time and space seemed to bow before her, and the hands of the clock ran on as quickly as her youthful daring.
—In Paris? said Cadignan.

Because it is so representative of Bernanos' first narrative manner, this passage arbitrarily selected from countless similar ones in this novel, deserves comment. Between Mouchette's defiant "Yes!" and Cadignan's quizzical "A Paris?", almost no narrative time elapses. Yet Bernanos himself momentarily suspends the progress of time to describe Mouchette's tormented emotional state. The imagery compounds the initial impression of almost hysterical confusion: ideas buzzing like a hive of bees, Mouchette's dizziness, the constantly vague plural of "a thousand lies," "an infinity of lies," "the endless chain." Every emotion surges forth only to fade into dream-like unreality. If narrative time has been artificially slowed by the intrusion of this passage, the psychic time in the character herself has been dramatically accelerated: the hands of the clock run rampant and the tempo is further increased by the chimerical vagueness of her emotions. The reader, though knowing intuitively what kind of emotional experience Bernanos is trying to convey, is at a loss to assign specific meaning even to words that seem analytical or conceptual. Of what relevance is the comparison of her burst of confidence to an effusion of life? A question which, strangely, the reader never asks. What matters here is that in this typically Bernanosian example of narrator's intervention, there is a unique abstract poetry, one, that is, whose subject is all but indefinable unless that subject *itself* be the ineffability of the experience. Of the novelists who dared to deal with mystical states, Dostoevsky alone relied on dialogue to lay bare the recesses of his characters' souls even when they were patently lying. Bernanos' generally resorts to a more traditional narrative method, that of a semi-poetic meditation on his characters' emotions as a ceremonial commentator watching his creations perform and intervening when their own words and gestures prove inaccurate or inadequate, or when their actions have a significance of which they themselves could not be aware. Only in *Journal d'un Curé de Campagne (Diary of a Country Priest)* and *M. Ouine,* will Bernanos experiment with a more objective 'modern' method.

When we first meet Mouchette, she has just entered the Malorthy home bearing a bucket of fresh milk. Almost immediately thereafter she faints, and her parents soon guess that she is pregnant. This initial vision is of crucial significance, for the story of Mouchette is that of the corruption of a completely natural being, a wild thing, a child, by Satan himself and by the Satanic forces of modern life represented by Malorthy, the Marquis and Dr. Gallet. Like Rimbaud ("my old comrade Rimbaud," Bernanos called him), Mouchette's adolescent imagination leads her to desperate rebellion against the straightjacket of bourgeois conventionality, to a thirst for freedom, adventure and love. Three times she will be imprisoned by her implacable foes: her father's house is likened to a cage; the Marquis locks her in his living-room; the doctor in his study. Twice she will escape; finally, flight from physical confinement is no longer enough. Mouchette must then escape from reality into madness and ultimately from life into death. She herself has become a Satanic creature, but one in whom vestiges of childhood purity (Bernanos constantly endows her with the adjective "petite") remain. Moreover, her complete devotion to evil paradoxically endows her with a vigorous and primitive integrity: she, not her tormentors, is destined for possible salvation. The pattern is a familiar one in Catholic novels. "The sinner is at the very core of Christianity. No one is as competent in matters of Christianity, unless it be the saint," Charles Péguy wrote in what was to become the epigraph to Graham Greene's *The Heart of the Matter.*

Mouchette's precipitous fall from grace began, a lyrical flashback tells us, one fine morning in the month of June when her mother told her to check on the cows grazing in the meadow. She was never to forget that bright morning and the marvelous vision she had at the edge of the woods of "her hero, smoking his briar, in his velvet jacket and heavy boots, like a king." She is a mirror of the landscape itself, in full flower, sixteen years old, nourishing within her "curiosity for pleasure and risk, like a ripening fruit." One is reminded of the medieval *pastourelle* and its ever recurring tale of the knight's encounter with the innocent shepherdess on the high road. The hapless maid had all she could do to resist the artful blandishments of her would-be seducer; there were never any serious consequences, at least not in the song. But in Bernanos' world the age of chivalresque honor is over: "We are no longer in the age of 'Seigneurs'," the Marquis jokingly tells Malorthy, referring only, he thinks, to the ancient *droit du seigneur.* The contrast between Mouchette's credulous childlike romanticism and the cynicism of the adult world has been superbly heightened by the structural position assigned to the important flashback of their meeting. It occurs immediately after the interview between Malorthy and Cadignan. The reader had already heard the pipesmoking republican brewer trying to make an advantageous deal with the pipesmoking, pleasure loving Marquis, who (a sure sign of his mediocrity in Bernanos' eyes) himself invokes the protection of the Republic's laws. The atmosphere of their meeting is that of a stand at a country market where two shrewd men are haggling over the price of livestock, each trying to dupe the other by expedient threats and lies. Ultimately, they get so entangled in the web of mendacity that they both feel duped by Mouchette herself. The meeting is inconclusive, though the pale blue eyes of the Marquis reflect his decision on a future course of action: "At that moment, Germaine could have seen her destiny inscribed there." Her encounter with the Marquis was not an innocent *pastourelle:* there *will* be consequences, and the fine fruit of Germaine's adolescence will become the flower of venom growing within her womb (images of decomposition will become a recurring symbol of evil in Bernanos' novels). For a time, the credulous child retains her illusions about her *knight.* When her father pretends that Cadignan has struck him, she has a flashing vision of her hero "in his superb anger." But soon these storybook notions, as Cadignan himself calls them, are dispelled. Mouchette's interview with the Marquis is merely an echo of her father's visit to the chateau. Now Cadignan is the one trying to strike a bargain, and his words repeat *verbatim* those of the brewer: "A vous de proposer" ("Your turn to bid.") Instead of a hero Mouchette has found a paunchy double of her own hated father, one whose reactions to her proposal of elopement are those of a cautious shopkeeper. Her disenchantment is complete: "I'd have thought you were a different kind of man." In her innocence, Mouchette had no doubt forgotten that when she met her "knight" on that luminous June morning, he had been accompanied by his prophetically named dogs *Roule-à-Mort* and *Rabat-Joie.* The Marquis' only real passion is hunting; Mouchette is but his prey.

Bernanos creates a complex network of imagery to emphasize poetically both the predatory quality of Cadignan and her untamed ferocity resulting from the defilement of her innocence. Escaping from the paternal abode, she is likened to a young female animal "trying out its adult muscles, its teeth and claws". During the course of her story she is variously described as a young wolf, a light doe, a supple beast. There are constant allusions to her curled-back lips, her sharp little teeth, the references becoming more frequent as her rebellion deepens. Cadignan, appropriately, speaks largely in the jargon of venery, telling Malorthy, for example, that his daughter "that nice bit of game . . . would drive a spaniel mad." Love, he says, is a cat-and-mouse game; the mouse is released only to be instantly recaptured. Mouchette is that mouse; each of her escapes leads to recapture, and it is this loss of freedom, that of the caged wild animal, which drives her to hysteria. Echoing Rimbaud, Bernanos depicts her as a child setting out to discover a new world only to find herself, at the end of a day of wandering, standing in front of the well in the family garden." 'Nothing has changed,' she murmured, 'there's nothing new' " (an ironic echo of the biblical source of the novel's title). Her anger is so intense that she breaks into that hysterical laughter which for Bernanos is the external sign of the Satanic presence. Here it foreshadows her nervous collapse at the end of the prologue. From a free spirit, she has been transformed into someone "possessed." Cadignan cannot understand her dreams. Always the hunter, he chases her around the room bearing her off "like a prey." He stalks her like "a skittish bird." But Mouchette is no longer the passive mouse of the game. In a burst of rage she grabs his finest gun from the wall, and when he continues to approach her "the way one does a dangerous dog," she fires. The pattern has been reversed: the hunter has become the hunted. His death is in no way sacrificial, however, For what *has* been sacrificed is the sacred childhood integrity of Mouchette's early dreams of revolt against her family's vulgar materialism and conventionality. From now on her wildness becomes a sign of Satan. Only much later in the novel will this savage creature meet a hunter truly worthy of her demonic energies. Father Donissan is "a hunter of souls." Mouchette is "the animal far from its lair." Bernanos, faithful to the novel's imagery, describes her as "his first prey."

The violation of the sacrosanct childlike spirit is, of course, a common theme in Christian literature. The rape of the feeble-minded swineherd Lisa, in *The Brothers Karamazov*, leads to the birth of the monster Smerdyakov. It is entirely appropriate therefore that Mouchette's child by Cadignan be still-born, and one wonders whether this dead baby is not also the symbol of the death of what was pure in Mouchette herself. Bernanos seems to have little concern for the moral and legal consequences of the murder itself. He is preoccupied primarily by the inner transformation resulting from the crime. Instead of rebellion, self-destruction becomes her goal in the confrontation with Dr. Gallet.

The Malorthy family is Bernanos' caricature of the ambitious tradesman class. After failing to strike a bargain with Cadignan, Malorthy looks proudly at his fine brick house, with its begonias and brewery, and decides that his twenty year wait to replace the Marquis as power in the village will soon be ended. An ardent defender of the Republic, Malorthy had wanted to name his daughter

Lucretia, but at the insistence of the village priest (the only time he is mentioned in the Prologue), he agreed to a more Christian name. Malorthy's anticlericalism in equally ridiculous. When his wife, a benign but evanescent figure, proposes that her adolescent daughter needs religious training, he rebuffs her angrily: "What does she need a priest for? to teach her in the confessional what she shouldn't know?" One of the reasons for her downfall may well be her lack of religious training. Bernanos cannot help mocking the tradesman and Republican, representative of what he as Catholic and royalist clearly despises, and once again ideology distorts novelistic psychology when Mouchette has republican scruples about loving a Marquis. A sixteen year-old girl full of storybook dreams of chivalresque romance would scarcely be troubled by such considerations.

Mouchette is made of the stuff of poets, heroes and fictional criminals. She is willing to dare, to take risks, to live, to face the world of the unknown. If her affair with Cadignan represents her first attempt to realize her dreams, it is her categorical refusal to obey her father's order to see Gallet which marks the high point of her rebellion against "good conduct which brings its own reward." Bernanos appropriately compares the bitter-sweetness of her first "no" to her first kiss. In her fantasies, Mouchette had already been an intrepid traveler. Unlike Columbus, she had sought an endless road, not a circular return (Bernanos' image), a road leading only to freedom: "She left behind all her past as one leaves a one night's shelter." But after the murder she returns under the family roof: what had been a cage ironically becomes a refuge from the law. Now the worm of boredom (since Baudelaire, the image of the modern sin) devours her youthful dreams, and she is on the inner road to despair. Her love for Cadignan had been her first "secret" (her predilection for this word is itself a sign of her childishness); her new secrets (the murder and her affair with Gallet) measure the change in her: "she loved him as the image and symbol of her own degradation." Ironically, Gallet sees *his* liaison with Mouchette as a liberation from the long humiliation of married life. The exertions of his renewed senses make him put on weight, while Mouchette, despite her pregnancy, wastes away in body and soul.

The concluding episode of "Histoire de Mouchette" has few rivals for brilliance of execution in all of Bernanos. It is as memorable as Cénabre's walk with the beggar in *L'Imposture* and the visit to the countess in *Journal d'un Curé de Campagne*. In this scene between Mouchette and Gallet, there are unmistakable echoes of her earlier interview with the Marquis. She has ostensibly come to announce her pregnancy and to find, by lying if necessary, an influential protector. Each time, she encounters misunderstanding and an unwillingness to take the slightest risk on her behalf. Violence becomes inevitable, though it will take appropriately different forms. In both scenes, she expresses her rage in unearthly sound: savage laughter at the chateau, "like a war cry"; in Gallet's study, "on one note alternately heavy and sharp, this superhuman lament resounds throughout the house." If both sounds recall the cry of a wild animal in a cage, there is a radical difference which is reflected in a change of imagery. Mouchette is no longer the graceful wild creature of the earlier scene; here she compares herself and her lover to odd centipedes who, diving in a pond, leave a cloud of mud. Bernanos has not forgotten the monster of the novel's opening paragraph.

Mouchette is desperately in need of the ministrations of the "republican's parish priest," since no other priest is available. The rapid accumulation of symptoms of impending mental breakdown are a mute and unconscious appeal for help; so is her confession. But the doctor is incapable of understanding ("the law is the law," he says). He offers only some learned medical jargon and some tranquillizing syrup from a pharmaceutical bottle. Her mother, Cadignan and now Gallet find her "mad enough to be committed." None of them can help; only the supernatural insight of a Father Donissan can illuminate the darkest recesses of a tortured possessed soul. What Bernanos implies here (he frequently caricatures psychiatrists) is that no mere psychic disturbance is responsible for Mouchette's disintegration, that insanity is but the surface reflection of the ineffable workings of Satan. What she is released from a rest home as "completely cured," her most acute crisis is still to come. Similarly, Father Donissan himself will be remanded for psychiatric treatment at the end of "La Tentation de Désespoir" by well-meaning Church authorities who are as uncomprehending as the bogus curate, Dr. Gallet. Mystical experiences, be they Satanic or angelic, have always been suspect in an age of positivism.

The doctor calls himself Mouchette's "friend and confessor," but when she recounts her dream of suicide by drowning he cruelly mimics her pathetic intonation. The detailed confession of the murder of Cadignan falls on wilfully deaf ears. She *hopefully* asks Gallet whether he believes in Hell, only to have her question treated as an idle joke. Belief in the reality of Satan would eventually imply belief in his divine opposite. Mouchette, without any awareness on her part, has taken this initial step toward faith; the very need to confess suggests that she is not irrevocably lost. Later, Donissan will say: "When the spirit of revolt was in you, I saw the name of God inscribed in your heart." But now her republican confessor, himself the very symbol of her degradation, is in no position to provide absolution. He is primarily, and indeed comically, concerned with external respectability. During the most shattering of Mouchette's crises, he refers constantly to the imminent arrival of his wife, a thought that inspires more fear in him than the idea of Hell. Since her incoherent outburst, Mouchette had been speaking with surprising lucidity, instinctively using every verbal and physical tactic in a desperate plea for help. But when the doctor deprives her of guilt for the murder, assuring her that no legal proof exists, she knows complete despair. She now has nothing, not even her crime. No words can convey this anguish; the mad howl of the caged beast is the only worthy lamentation. Many pages later, in "La Tentation du Désespoir," she will at last meet a confessor, in the person of Donissan, who not only is convinced of the reality of Satan but is willing to risk, to risk, indeed, his very salvation to redeem the soul of the childlike sinner.

From the very first, reviewers were offended by the apparently tenuous relationship of the prologue to the rest of the novel. The very order of composition (the prologue was written *after* the final section on "Le Saint de Lumbres," but before "La Tentation du Désespoir") is significant: it is thanks to Mouchette's meeting with Donissan in "La Tentation du Désespoir" that the prologue attains religious significance as a parable of demonic possession in a godless world, a world that does not believe in Hell because it *is* Hell. (And "Le Saint de Lumbres" would have been little more than hagiography with a poorly integrated admixture of satire, as we shall see in the next section, without the Prologue.) As Bernanos wrote in *Journal d'un Curé de Campagne,* "there is a communion of saints, there is also a communion of sinners." That world of sinners needs "the pure and chosen one," who can dispell the treacherous light of the false dawn of Lucifer. It was Mouchette's scream of despair, Bernanos later explained, which called Donissan into the novel. Yet the story of the future Saint of Lumbres needed the profane mode of "Histoire de Mouchette." "Poetry is nothing other than the song of our misery," Bernanos wrote in 1939. "Histoire de Mouchette" is the indispensable first stanza of that great lamentation.

B. *Hostile Phantoms:* Sous le Soleil de Satan *and* M. Ouine

No author could be more alien to the modern tradition of the creator-critic (exemplified by Baudelaire, T. S. Eliot, and Valéry) than Georges Bernanos. No one seems less preoccupied by purely esthetic problems. "No one is less art for art . . . than I," he wrote to his spiritual director Dom Besse. He has nothing but contempt for "literary literature composed and decomposed in an enclosed though transparent test-tube as in a chemical experiment." He protests at having to submit his writings piecemeal for editorial emendation: "If I had done that with *Sous le Soleil de Satan,* God knows what idiotic corrections would have been proposed—or imposed—which might have made the book one of those well-constructed novels." I inquired once of Father Pézeril, the executor of Bernanos' papers, whether there were any discussions of his conception of the art of the novel in the unpublished correspondence, and I was assured that the author of *M.Ouine* was not a man of letters! He was, nonetheless, an avid reader. His polemic works are replete with the names of major figures in modern literature; he judges them all, condemns most of them, but almost never on esthetic criteria. What counts is the writer's spiritual condition, his moral influence, the Catholic relevance of his subject matter ("My song is not immortal but its subject is!"). He admires Barbey and Bloy excessively, disdains Proust and Gide. When he wrote *Sous le Soleil de Satan,* he said in 1940, he had had the choice of pleasing or convincing and chose to convince.

And so that brilliant first novel is, as we have seen, patently flawed by the frequent, tasteless interventions of the polemicist. Perhaps the most flagrant false note (for those who care about the Jamesian tradition) is the introduction at the novel's end of a lengthy, apparently gratuitous caricature of Anatole France in the person of Antoine Saint-Marin of the French Academy, "the last of the Greeks," a character seemingly unrelated to the main lines of the story of Mouchette and Father Donissan, the drama of damnation and salvation. We have seen, however, that the section of the novel devoted to Saint-Marin, "Le Saint de Lumbres," was written *first*. If we reread the novel according to the initial order of creation, we have the uneasy feeling that the despised Saint-Marin is gazing malevolently and yet protectively at the melodramatic convulsions of Mouchette as well as at the metaphysical combat waged against Satan by Father Donissan, the future Saint of Lumbres.

The true motivation for Saint-Marin's strange pilgrimage to the Saint's parish church is never fully explained, but it is obvious that he is driven by intellectual curiosity, not by spiritual necessity. Like Anatole France, he prides himself on his Hellenism and was long hailed as "this new miracle of Mediterranean civilization" (he knows nothing of real miracles!). The young grammarians who form his entourage praise his "learned simplicity, his roué style," his "boulevard skepticism," his "intimate impertinence." The reputation of this self-styled "professor of doubt" had, like that of Anatole France, been consecrated by membership in the Franch Academy. Bernanos clearly delights in depicting Saint-Marin's lechery, his dependence on drugs, his un-Christian terror of death. But the words recurring most frequently in this memorable caricature are *skepticism* and *irony*, as clearly applicable to Anatole France as the appellation "old juggler," used perhaps to remind the reader of France's *Le Jongleur de Notre-Dame*. Accumulation of recognizable traits does not make this into a frivolous *roman à clef*, however. For Bernanos, Anatole France was the symbol of everything that was hateful in a dechristianized modern France living in the false light of Satan's Sun: "Our Athenian republic has made Anatole France its God," he wrote in *The Twilight of Old Men (Le Crépuscule des Vieux)*. "The 18th century is trying to make its comeback in his wake."

In an interview given shortly after the publication of his first novel, Bernanos, far from denying the original of Saint-Marin, launched into a new tirade:

> I didn't want to limit myself to a caricature of Anatole France, but since you mentioned him, so much the better. That must make his few disciples happy at a time when their master is meeting an indifference and oblivion even harder to take than scorn. His work is vile. It was only a game, you say. But what kind of game? To toy with man's hope is to play with the hunger and thirst of the poor. There is somewhere in the world today someone without hope just because the author of *Thaïs* had wit, knew his style. That is a sin without remission, the essential, absolute crime. Hatred itself yields to a kind of revulsion if one thinks that this consumption of hope only served to provide this cruel old man with the pleasures of a libertine professor. No! I don't hate him. I simply want to apply to him the anathema of the Gospel: It would be good had this man never been born.

It is obvious that the last lines of this vituperation echo, almost verbatim, passages in the portrait of Saint-Marin in the novel. But far more important to the novel is the attack on France, not as the defender of Dreyfus, but as the author of *Thaïs*. In *Sous le Soleil de Satan*, Saint-Marin is referred to with annoying frequency as the author of the *Paschal Candle*, the religious title of a characteristically ironic novel which becomes synonymous with *Thaïs*. "If you haven't yet seen the hermit," the doctor from Chevranches tells Saint-Marin, "at least you know the hermitage. What a strange house! What solitude!" As the author of the *Paschal Candle* approaches the confessional where the contorted dead body of the Saint of Lumbres is hidden, he thinks aloud' "I've got my saint now!" If indeed Saint-Marin had written his book about the hermit of Lumbres, he would have written *Thaïs*; Father Donissan would have become Father Paphnuce.

Thaïs is, of course, a veritable anthology of parodies ranging from Plato's *Banquet* to Flaubert's *Temptation of Saint-Anthony*. For Bernanos, it is primarily an attack on faith itself, on the Communion of Saints, and he would view it as a spurious mockery of the very type of priest who interested him the most in his first works, the "athlete of God," the fisher of souls. In his eclectic and master-fully elegant style, France tells the story of Father Paphnuce, abbot of Antinoe and the most uncompromising ascetic in the desert of the Thebaid. No one observed more rigorous fasts, no one wore rougher hairshirts, no one whipped himself as mercilessly to pre-clude even the possibility of demonic visitation. Among his many talents, France writes ironically, was the uncanny ability to distinguish dreams sent by God from those inspired by Satan. And so, despite the memories of his own Augustinian youth, Paphnuce sets out to Alexandria to convert the courtesan Thaïs whose image, stimulated by the priest's repressed sexuality (the author intimates) had been haunting his 'divinely' inspired dreams. Thaïs herself was born of poor, idolatrous tavern-keepers and after a childhood of abuse in an atmosphere of drunken debauchery runs away to become a dancer. She is not unready to listen to Paphnuce's arguments, for she has be-gun to worry about aging; nor has she forgotten the Christian slave Ahmes, who had had her baptized. But it is the banquet and the sub-sequent orgy which lead her to obey Paphnuce's entreaties to re-nounce her life of sin by following him into the desert to a convent: "Look, it is evening, my sister. The blue shadows of night cover the hillsides. But soon you will see the tabernacles of life shining in the sunrise, soon you will see the light of the roses of eternal morning." One can imagine Bernanos' reaction upon encountering in this ironic context a cluster of images which for him was replete with the most personal and intense significance. He returned incessantly to the image of night and dawn, so much so that for him Lucifer was "false dawn"; to console the sinner he wrote: "When one journeys to the end of the night, one will meet a new dawn."

The final section of *Thaïs* is the most blatantly satirical. "Saint" Paphnuce returns to the hermitage in the Thebaid, still haunted by the visions of Thaïs which by now have become far less ambiguous. The devil himself has entered his life, but ironically at the very moment that he joins the ranks of the possessed, crouch-ing on top of a phallic column, he becomes a saint in the public's view. Thousands flock to witness the hermit's ultimate act of self-mortification; a commercialized pilgrimage, not unlike Lourdes, flourishes on the spot. Finally, upon hearing that Thaïs is dying in

an aura of sanctity, Paphnuce resolves to yield to the devil's blandishments, only to learn to his horror that the sisters view him as a
diabolic vampire.

This rudimentary but necessary plot summary cannot help
but evoke certain resonances familiar to the student of Bernanos'
first novel. Like Paphnuce, Father Donissan is an obsessively rigorous
ascetic, whipping himself cruelly, wearing hairshirts and fasting.
Indeed, one of the sights which Saint-Marin finds most intriguing
at Lumbres is of "the cross, the leather whip, the bloody wall . . . "
Unfortunately, Bernanos' priest does not have the uncanny ability,
with which France roguishly endowed his hero, to distinguish divine
messages from demonic temptation. Donissan, like Paphnuce, sees
Satan everywhere, above all in his own soul, and each of his intended
miracles (especially the exorcism of Mouchette and the attempted
resurrection of the little Havret boy) turns out to have been the
result of diabolic complicity. "I also did some foolish things,"
Donissan admits to a priest reading aloud a chapter from the *Lives
of the Desert Fathers;* Paphnuce's extravagances, we remember,
are based on those same prodigious "Lives." Bernanos speculated
on his first novel: "One could imagine writing it romantically.
Donissan would be in open conflict with his bishop . . . Mouchette
would be a courtisane sanctified by vice and would give lessons to
the Pope and recite the monologue from *Ruy Blas* in the cathedral."
One thinks immediately of Thaïs. Even as Bernanos really created
her, Mouchette is in the mould of France's heroine. The daughter of
non-believing parents (her father is a brewer, Thaïs's ran a sailor's
tavern), she soon becomes the victim of Cadignan's sexual appetites,
falling thereafter into greater depravity complicated by severe mental
disorder until possible salvation appears in the person of Donissan.
Unlike Paphnuce's unctuous appeal for Thaïs' conversion,   clearly
a parody of edifying Church pamphleteering ("what shivers will
ripple through the flesh of your soul when you feel the fingers of
light touching your eyes!"), Donissan performs a full-fledged exorcism. Unlike Thaïs' facile conversion and passive ascension toward
sainthood, Mouchette's very salvation is in doubt despite her possible
conversion *in articulo mortis,* when she cuts her throat in satanic
despair. Finally, both Father Paphnuce and Father Donissan become

"saints" and their respective hermitages become the sites of "miracles" and subsequently the goal of pilgrimages.

It would be foolish to insist on further analogies of detail. What is of interest here, and in *M. Ouine,* is creation dictated by a hostile phantom. Though the life of the Curé d'Ars, *Les Diaboliques* of Barbey and the polemic 'novels' of Bloy would seem to most Bernanos scholars more abundant preserves for source-hunting, his reaction to *Thaïs* informed his first novel. Since *Thaïs* is itself a parody, Bernanos could not himself parody France's novel (though *L'Imposture* was to show him capable of vicious *ad hominem* parody). Instead he wrote what one might call counter-parody. Where France made fun of the demon-haunted priest, Bernanos took him seriously and transformed his nightmarish existence into a spiritual drama worthy of Dostoevsky. Both priest-heroes are extremists, however, and the image of the priesthood projected by Donissan is thoroughly disconcerting to literal-minded Catholic readers. Where the French skeptic parodied the Romantic repentant Magdalena topos, Bernanos treated the fall and possible redemption of Mouchette with high seriousness; where France cleverly mocked the commercialized pilgrimages of Fatima and Lourdes, Bernanos, while equally contemptuous of popular cure hunting, portrayed a genuine, if misguided, "saint." In *Sous le Soleil de Satan* Bernanos was still groping with the rudiments of novelistic craft, and "Le Saint de Lumbres," with its esthetically unpardonable creation of Saint-Marin (who detracts from the effect of Donissan's death), was his admission that his first novel was written not only under Satan's sun but in the half-light of Anatole France's irony.

M. Ouine

Those to whom [Bernanos] spoke at this time of his novel remember he presented it as a satire of André Gide—the man who says 'yes' and 'no' at the same time. Of this first intention, almost nothing remains in the final work where it is only too obvious that the character of Ouine owes most to interior sources.

Albert Béguin

If, as Béguin alleges, almost nothing of the original personal satire of Gide remains, it is because Bernanos had by now (he worked on the novel from 1931 to 1940) become a skillful novelistic technician who would never again allow a work to be flawed by gross personal caricature. What has happened, I think, is that Bernanos has moved from parody *ad hominem* to parody *ad opus;* that is, Gidian ideas, themes and even phrases are incorporated into *M. Ouine,* so that the novel which Bernanos' called "Job's dungheap" remains a response to the hostile voice of the author of *L'Immoraliste* despite Béguin. For Gide's very name is anathema to Bernanos: in the articles of the 1920's and 1930's, collected in *Le Crépuscule des Vieux,* Bernanos rails constantly against Gide and his disciples: "We saw them swarming around M. Gide and clutching to the old wormy tree-trunk like a swarm of gray flies when the first hard frost of winter comes."

The image of Gide which dominates Bernanos' vituperations is that of the teacher, the corrupter of youth, the didactic poet of *Les Nourritures terrestres,* and the arbiter of literary taste. Bernanos sees French youth with "its diploma in immoralism," becoming servile imitators of their master's homosexuality while remaining afraid of life itself, "dying before being able to flower in the corpse where they were hatched." Gide's self-proclaimed pedagogical mission as a liberator of youth from moral constriction so infuriates Bernanos that he speaks of him as the "spiritual pimp for a little troop of rebellious archangels who need their arses wiped." "That old poisonous crone," "that mummy preserved in herbs," Gide is like "the primitive animals for whom one orifice serves as mouth and anus, the last word in Gidian sincerity." These are some of the endearing epithets Bernanos applies to the author of *Les Faux-Monnayeurs.* But above all, he attacks Gide's unwillingness to take a stand, to assume the Bernanosian—or Pascalian— risk ("Old people fear error less than risk," we read in *Sous le Soleil de Satan*). "The predilection of the pious immoralist was to stir up souls by learned equivocation . . . at the precise juncture where shame (which this strange man seems to crave) is born." For Bernanos, André Gide is the man who says both "Oui" and "Non": OUINE.

In the light of these vicious polemics, it is revealing that Bernanos stresses M. Ouine's role as spiritual mentor, as self-designated pedagogue. He is a retired professor of Modern Languages who has devised a new method of teaching which has won the attention of the ministry. He recalls with pleasure that "there is not one of my students who has not dreamed of following me to the end of the earth." His chosen disciple in the dead parish of Fenouille is the young boy Philippe, who considers Ouine "the predestined companion for life, the initiator, the hero traced through so many books." He calls Ouine "master." The 'professor' expresses himself constantly in Gidian aphorisms: "This room . . . it is I who wanted its austerity" (dénuement); "each of us can go to the very depth of himself"; " . . . I float and absorb. We shall teach you the secret of letting yourself be filled by the passing hour." Like Gide, or at least like Bernanos' conception of him, Ouine's essential moral posture is ambiguous. A priest remarks that he has never heard from him a word either for or against religion: "He's only interested in moral problems." Late in the novel, the author comments that Ouine was incapable of renouncing "even one of those hours which mark progress toward deliverance and total freedom; he remembers hating only one constraint, that of good and evil, etc." Moreover, in a rather insidious manner, Bernanos allows himself to make certain allusions to Gide's work ("which of us is not seeking the lost sheep?"); or to Gide's person: "M. Valéry, for example, the former tax collector, your master and he used to be friends," someone tells Philippe. There are disturbing undertones of homosexuality in Ouine's friendship with Philippe: "those beautiful shaped hands which do both good and evil like those of a god," Jambe-de-Laine tells the boy. It is alleged, moreover, that Ouine killed the crippled cowherd.

More revealing than a list of details identifying Gide with Ouine is a study of the evolution of the teacher-disciple relationship. In Gide's work this is, of course, a recurring pattern. Ménalque and Nathanaël in *Les Nourritures*, Ménalque and Michel in *L'Immoraliste*, Edouard and Bernard in *Les Faux-Monnayeurs*. In *M. Ouine*, what Bernanos has done is to dramatize the pernicious influence that an old immoralist might have had on a young would-be André Gide! Philippe's childhood surrounded by women cannot help but recall Gide's autobiography, *Si le grain ne meurt (If it die)*, and *La Porte étroite (Strait is the Gate)*. He lives with his mother and an English governess of sorts named "Miss"; his father is either dead or has disappeared (so much is ambiguous in *M. Ouine*). But instead of the apparently tranquil, harmonious and modest existence of an Anna Shackleton, Bernanos's version of Gide's governess is, it is hinted darkly, involved in a lesbian relationship with Philippe's mother. And her dealings with "Steeny" (she calls him that after her favorite English novel) is itself full of erotic undertones. Madame de Néréis, the insane *châtelaine* of Wambescourt with whom Ouine is staying, comments on Philippe's resemblance to his master and to prove her point pulls out an old picture of Ouine as a student:

> What in the world could Philippe have in common with this ridiculous boy? The gaze, no doubt. And suddenly, as though through the faded paper a double shadow moves, backward, backward, shrinking into imperceptible pupils, now almost vanished, to two small pale dots which fix on Steeny with a kind of imperious sadness. "My eyes!" he thinks. "exactly my eyes!"

Philippe tears up the picture, but Madame de Néréis continues to insist on its importance, recounting that Ouine had said of the boy: "I have just seen myself, like a dead man looking into the past. The little boy I used to be, I saw him, I could have touched him . . . " With astonishing rapidity Ouine's young disciple becomes a virtual replica of the master himself. Steeny's predisposition toward becoming a new Gide is such that in the course of his first meeting with Ouine he already expresses himself in thoroughly Gidian terms: "I am suspicious of God, that is the way I worship him." Or: "I follow my inclination *(pente)* that is all."

The ill-fated cowherd who hears Steeny's various admonitions to live life spontaneously comments: "I am sure that you have just spoken exactly like he (Ouine) does; I wouldn't have recognized your voice." Like Gide's Bernard Profitendieu, indeed like the departing Prodigal himself, Steeny exults in being fatherless: "No more ancestors, the world begins anew. I prefer that." He will take to the open road, but he runs straight from his road to the monastically furnished room of "that paunchy half-god," as Bernanos contemptuously labels Ouine.

The death of the eponymous hero is Bernanos' cruelest revenge on the man he considered to be the perverter of French youth.

The retired professor of languages, who had functioned as anti-priest or negative saint, causing moral disintegration, suffering and even crime in "the dead parish" (Bernanos' first title for the book was *La Paroisse morte*), will die fully aware of his own insignificance: "I am nothing." To his bewildered disciple he tells the extraordinary myth of the empty bottle, drawing his symbol from the very bottle which he had shared with Steeny in a bizarre ceremony of consecration in evil in the early pages of the novel. "I am empty too," he admits. He had thirsted for souls like a bogus God, he had won disciples, contaminated an entire parish, but in so doing, Ouine, like the Gide of Bernanosian polemics, lost his own soul. If Gide's works were "the delectations of an imagination that was always mediocre but today is impotent, unable to excrete its dreams," that mediocrity provided an impulse for Bernanos' most ambitious novel. He was aware of this notion of creative counter-attack when he wrote to a more benign adversary, the poetess Anna de Noailles, in 1926: "I cannot open one of your books without blushing because I have never let you know that they have long been my familiar enemies . . . and that one of the goals of my poor life is to give you up entirely." The tension between polemicist and novelist in Bernanos's writing was such that he often began with a counter-attack on an enemy before creating his own memorable characters. *L'Imposture* is a bad novel precisely because it is almost exclusively caricatural; only the presence of Abbé Chevance saves that work. But in both *Sous le Soleil de Satan* and *M. Ouine,* his first and last novels, the direct polemic against the hostile phantoms is distilled into novelistic vision.

C. Un Mauvais Rêve: *Bernanos and Dostoevsky*

"Do you think this is a good time for such ridiculous behavior? You might just as well be in a Russian novel . . . " Philippe, a young malcontent and amateur terrorist, has just botched his first attempt at suicide (his second will be successful) and is now playfully pressing the cold, shiny revolver against the forehead of his friend and double, Olivier Mainville. The scene takes place in a crumbling boarding-house, the headquarters for an obscure international anarchist cell in a sordid Parisian faubourg; the novel is Bernanos' posthumously published *Un Mauvais Rêve (Night is darkest).* For most readers the explicit allusion to the Russian novel was hardly necessary; the echoes of Kirilov's extravagant suicide and of Peter Verkhovensky's meetings with his revolutionary group in *The Possessed* are unmistakable here. In the second part of *Un Mauvais Rêve*, we shall follow Simone Alfieri as she plans and executes a familiarly motivated, highly Dostoevskian murder:

> Of all the means she had devised for her deliverance, crime remained the final one within her reach, and commensurate with her impotent revolt. The victim was immaterial. The motive even more so. It was enough that her pride was flattered; she certainly would not have killed for the sake of robbery . . . whereas a long premeditated murder, carried out in cold blood, ruthlessly embarked on, brings about, at the fairest price, the complete and final break with man's society and its despicable order. It is a form of suicide but lacking the immediate fall, the dizzy descent toward nothingness. At least it allows a respite, however short; even if it is only long enough to allow a brief enjoyment of that holy solitude, the solitude of happiness or genius.

Simone beats the old lady of Souville to death with an andiron, then rummages frantically in the dresser drawers looking for money until she is chilled by the sound of someone rattling the front-door chain. Two hours later, after hiding in a back room, she can at last escape. In this scene Simone Alfieri becomes the Bernanosian Raskolnikov, (as the above plot similarities clearly show).

In an earlier novel, *La Joie* of 1928, a sinister Russian chauffeur, appropriately christened Fiodor, tears open his shirt with a violent gesture, showing five deep bullet marks. He had faced a firing-squad in Russia in front of a school-house: "I who am speaking to you, the five rifle barrels a few steps off (I could almost have touched them), and the snow was red with blood . . . What man ever saw his end nearer, face to face?" This haunting memory, which Fiodor calls "more sacred to me than my own mother," appears to be a reminiscence of an episode from Dostoevsky's life: that harrowing confrontation with a Czarist firing-squad in 1849, which found its way with such obsessive regularity into his novels.

No reader of Bernanos' works can fail to discern its Dostoevskian resonances, and indeed the major Bernanos critics, especially

Luc Estang in his *Présence de Bernanos,* have linked the two writers. But comparisons have remained conjectural, non-literary. I believe one is entitled to be more precise, witness a letter I received in 1964 from the late Robert Vallery-Radot, the French Catholic writer turned Trappist at Briquebec, to whom *Sous le Soleil de Satan* was dedicated and who was Bernanos' initial sponsor and life-long friend and confidant:

> It was above all at the time he was writing *La Joie* that he spoke to me of Dostoevsky. He ranked *The Brothers Karamazov* above all his novels, and he read it and reread it very closely during this period. I think of Ravel writing his *Hommage to Rameau* (Vallery-Radot means Debussy . . .); Fiodor, in *La Joie,* is like Bernanos' homage to the genius of Dostoevsky. He must have penetrated *The Idiot* to its very depths. Bernanos entered the Dostoevskian atmosphere and felt right at home.

If, as Vallery-Radot wrote elsewhere, Bernanos read primarily "to rediscover the dream which possessed him," he must truly have felt at home in reading Dostoevsky. Both writers, for example, shared a predilection for essentially melodramatic plot constructions. Guy Gaucher estimates that there are nine murders, twelve suicides and fourteen narrated death agonies in Bernanos' fiction; a necrological tally of Dostoevskian violence would be even more imposing. Beyond such rather haphazard resemblances, there seem to me to be subtler harmonies of intention and execution which may help to explain Bernanos' elective affinity for the Russian master.

In an important interview that took place in 1926, that is, shortly after the publication of *Sous le Soleil de Satan,* Bernanos himself provides a valuable clue, one which incredibly has not attracted critical attention:

> In a sense, everything remains to be written, everything! A man of great talent could redo from this point of view (the Catholic point of view) all of Dostoevsky's work, for example, or even Balzac's. As Vallery-Radot recently said to an editor of the Cahiers de Louvain, the Catholic novel is not one which only speaks to us of worthy sentiments, it is one where the existence of faith clashes with the passions. One must make as perceptible as possible the

tragic mystery of salvation. Listen: I would like to express by an image what I am thinking of. Let us take the characters of Dostoevsky, those he himself calls "The Possessed." We know the diagnosis of them offered by the great Russian. But what would have been the diagnosis of the Curé d'Ars, for example? What would *he* have seen in those dark souls?

In response to this statement, a fruitful approach to Bernanos' work is to consider it as his attempt to offer a Roman Catholic illumination of the shadowy souls of 'the possessed.' And the clairvoyant Curé d'Ars of Bernanos' hypothesis, the priest who, as he was fond of saying, learned of sin only from the mouths of sinners, is variously represented by Father Donissan, Abbé Chevance (in *L'Imposture*), and the Curate of Ambricourt (in *Journal d'un curé de campagne*), Catholic sacerdotal modulations of Dostoevsky's secular saints, Shatov, Prince Myshkin and Alyosha Karamazov. "Why, Prince," someone says to Myshkin, "your simplicity and innocence are such as were never heard of in the golden age, and then, all of a sudden, you pierce a fellow through and through, like an arrow, with such profound psychological insight." As Myshkin reads faces, so do Donissan and Ambricourt read the souls of Mouchette and Chantal; and their own simplicity and innocence match the 'Idiot's'.

The possessed who are to be succoured by Bernanos' Curé d'Ars figures are remarkably Dostoevskian too. The most tragic manifestation of the demonic presence, that is of becoming 'possessed,' can be found when innocent creatures are violated (sexually or intellectually) by one who is already among the possessed. "It is written in your book," Stavrogin says to Father Tikhon, pointing to the Gospels, "that there is no greater crime than to defile one of these little children." This is, of course, what Stavrogin has been doing throughout the novel. Not only does he confess to raping a young girl (the long expurgated scene in Father Tikhin's quarters); he also contracts an outrageous parody of a marriage with a potentially saintly figure, the feeble-minded virgin, Mary Lebyatkin, and interferes cruelly in the psychic life of Lisa Tushin. The results of his activities soon become apparent: Mary passes from holy simple-mindedness into the hysterical laughter which is the surest sign of the diabolic presence (in both *The Brothers Karamazov* and *Sous le*

Soleil de Satan, when the devil appears he is laughing); and Lisa herself "had suddenly started laughing, at first quietly and intermittently, then her laughter grew more uncontrollable, louder and more audible." One need only adduce "Histoire de Mouchette," where, we remember, the childlike mistress of Cadignan "bursting into laughter . . . drinking in her own sonorous defiance, filling the four corners of the old hall with a crystal tone that could have been a war cry." The Dostoevskian cast of Bernanos' novelistic imagination is clear. Totsky's seduction of Nastasya Filippovna in *The Idiot* pushes her toward insanity in the same way that Mouchette will yield to what the cynical Dr. Gallet terms hyperesthesia. As Mrs. Shatov's baby by Stavrogin will die, so does Mouchette give birth to a still-born child. And both Mouchette and the young victim of Svidrigailov's lust in *Crime and Punishment* will commit suicide. The pattern is relentlessly sustained in other Bernanos novels. There is the savage murder of Chantal de Clergerie by the chauffeur Fiodor in *La Joie*; in *L'Imposture* we learn that the evil writer Guérou "devours" young girls; in *Nouvelle Histoire de Mouchette,* the heroine is raped and subsequently drowns herself in a pond.

The importance of laughter as a recurring sign of the satanic in the works of the two novelists can be traced to a fundamental kinship. Both create an imposing roster of characters who, when humiliated or contaminated spiritually or physically, react perversely, rebelling against the integrity of their own personality. "We're ashamed," Mouchette says, "but between us, since the first day, have we been looking for anything else?" Dostoevsky calls them "self-lacerators." They frenetically debase themselves in public, but their suffering originates in pathological pride and fear, not in true humility. It is *unregenerative suffering.* To name but a few, Father Karamazov, Katerina Ivanovna, Nastasya Filippovna and the Underground Man join Pernichon of *L'Imposture,* the grandmother in *La Joie,* the Chantal of the country priest's diary, and Jambe-de-Laine in *M. Ouine* in this classification. The night Abbé Cénabre realizes he has lost his faith he hears himself laughing uncontrollably, much as Raskolnikov is constantly confronted with the convulsive laughter of his double Svidrigailov. The use of the double motif is closely linked to an almost manichean view of the world. Cénabre's walk with the beggar cannot help but recall Stavrogin's meeting with

Fedka. The various self-lacerators are usually just on this side of insanity and often do indeed lapse into madness or suicide. The madness of Cénabre at the end of *La Joie* or of Olivier Mainville in *Un Mauvais Rêve* is no less symbolic of spiritual corruption than the brain fever of Stavrogin and Ivan Karamazov. And psychiatry is not the remedy to purify the tainted soul. Porfiry's psychologizing only postpones Raskolnikov's acceptance of the cross; the modern theories of Dmitri Karamazov's defense lawyer miss the point entirely. The psychiatrists in Bernanos' novels, Lipotte and Lapérouse, are equally ineffectual, though they are equipped with the latest theories. For Dostoevsky and Bernanos, Alyosha's kiss to Ivan and Father Donissan's absolution of Mouchette provide the only form of redemptive therapy.

The self-lacerator expresses himself in uncontrolled, almost hysterical verbalizing. For both our novelists, saintly figures are essentially silent listeners, born confessors. Donissan, when he has become the Saint of Lumbres spends most of his waking hours in the confessional; and the Alyoshas, Myshkins, and Sonya Marmeladovs magnetically attract the confessions of the possessed. One might also, in more specifically ecclesiastical terms, point to Father Tikhon and Father Zossima. In contrast, the briefest excerpt from the endless monologues of the self-lacerators would show that by talking too much they invariably end up by lying. Lebedev, in *The Idiot*, explains that he lies from self-abasement; and Bernanos comments on Simone's lies in *Un Mauvais Rêve* that "long before drugs, lying had been for her another marvellous escape, an always effective relaxation, rest, oblivion." The cast of pathological liars is too imposing to permit listing here. But both writers comment extensively on the phenomenon, Dostoevsky in his *Diary of a Writer* and Bernanos in his projected preface to *L'Imposture*.

Drugs and alcohol provide further escape from *ennui* into an artificial paradise that turns inevitably into a real hell. In his essay, *La Liberté pour quoi faire (Freedom, to what end?)*, Bernanos calls toxicomania "that perverse form of escape, of fleeing one's own personality." If the Bernanos novels include among the most notable addicts Lapérouse in *La Joie*, Dr. Laville in the *Journal*, Dr. Lipotte, Philippe, Olivier and Simone in *Un Mauvais Rêve*, a list of the drunkards in Dostoevsky's works (for alcohol serves an analogous function for the Russian) would be impossibly long. "I drink in order to suffer," Marmeladov says. For both novelists, the desperate attempt to escape one's self ultimately leads to a far more tragic confrontation. It is no accident that Mouchette (in *Sous le Soleil*) kills herself in front of a mirror. "It is easier than one thinks to hate oneself," the Curé d'Ambricourt writes. "Grace comes from forgetting oneself. But even if all pride in us had died, the grace of graces would be to love oneself with humility."

If I were to point out the one trait which most clearly confirms the fraternity of vision here it would be a fundamentally Romantic mistrust of the intellect. "Evil comes from the constantly working brain, that monstrous animal, formless and flabby in its sheath like a worm, tireless pumper. Yes, why think?" This, from *M. Ouine*. For both writers, the intellectual is, almost by definition, the first to succumb to the temptation of knowledge; the picking of that forbidden fruit is what Conor Cruise O'Brien has called the religious Faust motif. Abbé Cénabre is less a priest than an historian. He fulfills his sacramental functions at the reserve desk of the *Bibliothèque nationale;* M. Ouine, we remember, is a retired professor. Both novelists reserve the most strident satirical tones of their lyre for intellectuals. Dostoevsky's hatred of a Rakitin or a Lebeziatnikov is matched by Bernanos' undisguised animus against Monsieur de Clergerie or Lapérouse. Writers in partucular, it would seem, betray not only religion but country. Interestingly, Anatole France and Turgenev, models for Saint-Marin (in *Sous le Soleil*) and Karamazinov (in *The Possessed*), are both essentially cosmopolitan and ironic. And André Gide (*M. Ouine*) is the very symbol of the deracinated intellectual.

Alyosha Karamazov and the Curé d'Ambricourt both state in identical words that hell is "not to love any more," and it is precisely the intellectual who is least able to love. "A real writer can't have children," the writer Ganse says in *Un Mauvais Rêve*. Children are pure, holy creatures. What intellectuals produce are monsters; Ivan creates Smerdiakov; Stepan Verkhovensky fathers Peter; M. Ouine forms *Jambe-de-Laine;* Ganse moulds Philippe and Olivier. "Truth is only spoken by people who are not smart," Ferdyshenko states in *The Idiot*. This, to paraphrase Nietzsche, makes all intellectuals liars.

"What would the Curé d'Ars have seen in these obscure souls?" Bernanos had asked in his 1926 interview. Though his priest-heroes do illuminate the tormented souls of the possessed, it has been the function of the novelist himself to provide the coherent diagnosis. But Bernanos' stated intention to redo Dostoevsky's *Possessed* from a Catholic point of view leads him to transform the Russian's saint-like figures (Shatov, Prince Myshkin, Alyosha Karamazov) into specifically Roman Catholic expressions: Donissan, Chevance, Chantal de Clergerie, the Curé d'Ambricourt. The consanguinity of these child-like, holy creatures has often been pointed out. They neglect the sacraments in favor of person-to-person soul fishing; they are all religious modulations of Romantic poet-heroes. Their natural habitat is the monastery, even the sanatorium; in the infernal world their best intentioned actions go astray and, typically, the interventions of a Donissan and a Myshkin have equally nefarious results. There is an important distinction between Dostoevsky and Bernanos with regard to their saint figures, however, one which shows that the Frenchman has indeed met his self-imposed challenge of "Catholicizing" Dostoevsky. For the Russian, the only path toward the regeneration of the sinner leads through suffering, and those of his novels where redemption remains a possibility are, as we have seen in Chapter II, open-ended, projecting into an unwritten future. Bernanos, on the other hand, believes in the sudden, mystical intervention of Grace, effected in part by the sacrificial act of the Saint ("sacrifice", etymologically, means *making holy*). Myshkin returns to his sanatorium in Switzerland, but Chantal de Clergerie's murder may have led Cénabre back to God; Shatov's death does not redeem his murderers or even Stavrogin, but the Curé d'Ambricourt's death may have restored a measure of faith to the defrocked priest, M. Dufréty, who gives him absolution. This is thematic, however; I have discussed the similarity of narrative strategies, the unnarrated 'future.' If the word which best represents Sonya Marmeladov, as she accompanies the sinner Raskolnikov to Siberia on the stations of his long itinerary of redemption, is *compassion (suffering with)*, the word for the Bernanosian Saint imitating Christ by dying (as Rayner Heppenstall has shown) as a scapegoat is *passion*.

Though in this constant process of comparison I have drawn many equal signs, I have not intended them to be qualitative equal signs. It is significant that *The Possessed* is the only Dostoevsky novel mentioned by Bernanos himself, for this work betrays precisely those uncertainties of narrative posture which were to plague Bernanos until he solved the dilemma (or repressed his polemical energies) in the first-person *Journal d'un curé de campagne* and in the objectified scenic techniques of *M. Ouine.* One might apply to Bernanos a characteristic remark which Max Jacob made to Charles Vildrac in 1910: "Ah! what a fine Russian novelist you would have made, had you been Russian!"

D. "A Certain Idea of France": Bernanos and De Gaulle

"Your rightful place is with us," General De Gaulle cabled Bernanos in Brazil in the most persuasive of his telegrams urging the novelist's return to the liberated Paris of 1945. And so, on May 30, Bernanos bid adieu to the youth of Brazil, but vowed that his renewed intimacy with France would only strengthen his ties to his war-time hosts:

> All that I will see again in my homeland, its cities, villages, rivers, highways, the old stone church, the fields cultivated for centuries, the ageless oak trees whose blessed shade no longer belongs to nature but to men, yes, everything I will see again will give me a lesson of fidelity, everything I will see again continues through the centuries to bear witness *for* that which is durable *against* whatever is forgotten, abandoned, foresworn. The creation of a great people is a miracle of faithfulness.

Upon his return Bernanos found that the *pays réel* dear to Maurras and to his own youthful royalism ("I dreamed of saints and heroes, neglecting the intermediary forms"), that "eternal France", had become the France of 1945, with its flourishing black market, its reconstituted but still squabbling multi-party system, its poisonous lies ("a cheaters' world"). The weight of exile, Bernanos understood after six unhappy months in Paris, is less burdensome in a foreign land than at home. Soon, despite his infirmity, Bernanos was to resume his nomadic wanderings, keeping the illusory vision of *le pays réel* real by avoiding the reality. And in so doing, he would follow the example of self-imposed exile given by another visionary committed to the idea of France and unwilling to accept its mediocre reality.

In *Le Figaro* for 2 February 1946, Bernanos wrote:

> Let's be frank. The Liberator of the Fatherland has just left for the same reasons which prompt thousands of young Frenchmen to ask for their passport.
>
> In the course of an interview—but interviews are not my strong-point—I said to General De Gaulle that the mediocre would finally win out over him, that they win out over everyone.

We know from his entreaties to the exile to return that De Gaulle admired Bernanos, but we know little more than that. We can, however, trace the crescendo of admiration for De Gaulle in Bernanos' writings, beginning with the first tentative mention, in January 1942, of "the now legendary soldier to whom every Frenchman worthy of the name has entrusted his hope, honor and revenge. General De Gaulle hasn't cheated. He accepted the burden of risk at the critical moment." Bernanos could only go by the General's speeches and actions (De Gaulle's *Mémoires* were published long after the novelist's death), yet his intuitive and poetic reaction to History destined to become "an adventure novel with colored pictures which makes little girls dream and boys shout with joy" will allow him from 1942 until the months just preceding his death in 1948 to move toward so complete a personal identification with De Gaulle and 'a certain idea of France' that among his very last writings are an extraordinary series of six *Messages imaginaires* entitled "The General speaks to you," published in *L'Intransigeant* from March through May 1948.

It is ironic that the advocate of the modernized, mobile army, the creator of the *force de frappe*, the initiator of the reign of the technocrats, should share a vision of France with the nostalgic Romantic and quixotic reactionary, the pamphleteer of a "France of saints, heroes and poets." But if we survey the structure of De Gaulle's

Mémoires, we find that it is in those pages where he becomes the man of the Word, rather than the narrator of deeds and the witness of his own actions, that he expresses his idea of France. That is, we must look to the openings and to the closing perorations of chapters and volumes and to those speeches which are public exhortations in a predicatory mode; there, the *poet* takes over from the *doer,* the politician and strategist; there the intense fraternity of vision linking De Gaulle to Bernanos becomes startlingly apparent.

> Toute ma vie, je me suis fait une certaine idée de la France. Le sentiment me l'inspire aussi bien que la raison. Ce qu'il y a, en moi, d'affectif imagine naturellement la France, telle la princesse des contes ou la madone aux fresques des murs, comme vouée à une destinée éminente et exceptionnelle. J'ai, d'instinct, l'impression que la Providence l'a créée pour des succès achevés ou des malheurs exemplaires. S'il advient que la médiocrité marque, pourtant, ses faits et gestes, j'en éprouve la sensation d'une absurde abnomalie, imputable aux fautes des Français, non au génie de la patrie.

> All my life, I have had a certain idea of France. Feeling inspires that as well as reason. My emotional side naturally imagines France, like the fairy-tale princess or the madonna on a frescoes wall, as dedicated to an eminent and exceptional destiny. Instinctively, I have the impression that Providence created France for out-and-out successes or exemplary misfortunes. If it transpires that mediocrity characterizes her deeds and actions, I feel there is an absurd abnomaly due not to the genius of the fatherland but to the errors of the French.

The temporal structure of that famous opening sentence may intentionally echo Proust's, but what counts is the insistence on the continuously ideated presence of the past in the present: *idée, sentiment, inspire, d'affectif, imagine.* De Gaulle's certain idea comes from the world of art, the fairy-tale princess or the madonna, idealization by the original creator surviving in a vision of History as form in the mind of the memorialist. I have already (in Chapter I) quoted some of the virtually limitless analogues in the work of the creator of Olivier Tréville-Sommerange, that novelist of "Old France, that is, of France herself, for a thousand years of history cannot be erased by 150 years of unfortunate fumbling." De Gaulle's notion of a

providential mission of exemplary suffering finds its counterpart in
Bernanos' 1940 affirmation that heroes are made through mis-
fortune, especially French heroes:

> Our only popular epic, *The Song of Roland,* is the history of a
> defeat; ten centuries ago the hearts of boys and girls of my race
> beat for a conquered child, dying with his face toward the enemy,
> one hand raised toward the angels, the other humbly seeking to
> grasp his friend's. Such is the inevitable choice of French honor.

And, of course, the word médiocrité, which both Bernanos and De
Gaulle apply incessantly to the multiparty regime of the 4th Republic, will, in the fulminations of the exiled novelist, be supplanted by
imbécilité, with a bitter disdain more becoming to an unheeded
prophet in the Brazilian wilderness than to a sometime exile at
Colombey-les-deux-Eglises.

De Gaulle's fidelity to 'a certain idea of France' is based on
at least five tenets of faith which he shares with Bernanos. "There is
no France without the sword" restates the General's view of French
origins as fashioned militarily, with the *fleur-de-lys,* symbol of
national unity, owing its origins to the three-pronged javelin. In his
Lettre aux Anglais, Bernanos asks rhetorically (on behalf of someone
who will never understand France): "What do the three innocent
lilies on its blue blazon have to do with the oldest military nation in
Europe?" He goes on to evoke France as "a military peasantry" and
to regret "the decline of military Christianity," (the old quixotic
refrain which we have sounded in a European perspective in Chapter I.
One thinks immediately of certain incarnations of the ideal in his
novels, especially Olivier in the *Journal.* As for De Gaulle, at the
very moment he is outlining the benefits of the *Plan* (the mechanized
modern France against which Bernanos was to inveigh in his praise
of *La France contre les robots*), De Gaulle's reflective fidelity insists
on the "other side of the medal": "that thousand-year old France,
whose nature, activity and genius have made it essentially rural . . .
How can one not understand that France herself and the great
changes in the works inevitably arouse the peasantry's suspicion and
melancholy?"

The goal of harmony among European nations leads from nostalgia for the Christian empire of the Middle Ages to the cathedral at Reims:

> symbol of our ancient traditions, but also the stage for so many clashes between hereditary enemies from the old Germanic invasions to the battles of the Marne. In the cathedral whose wounds have not yet healed, the French and German premiers unite their prayers to insure that on both sides of the Rhine the works of friendship replace forever the sorrows of war.

Each time that De Gaulle moves from his chronicling of progress under the Fifth Republic to the more oratorical passages, his nostalgia for Ancient France and his resentment against "a mechanized and urbanized France" register in a Bernanosian rhetorical tonality:

> To France, to Our Lady France, we can only say one thing, that nothing matters to us except serving her. We have to liberate her, beat the enemy, chastize the traitors, maintain her friendships, tear the gag from her mouth and the chains from limbs so that her voice may be heard as she resumes her fateful course. We ask her for nothing unless, perhaps, it be to beg her on the day of freedom to open her arms maternally to us so that on her bosom we may cry for joy, or on the day of our death to bury us gently in her good and holy earth.

Malraux is undoubtedly correct in stating that for De Gaulle, faith, like France herself, was a basic given: "but he loves to speak of France, he does not like to discuss his faith." For De Gaulle, "Our Lady France" inspires a parareligious vocabulary, with the leader in a position analogous to Bernanos' priests tracking their prey. Soldiering is a vocation, the leader embarks on "an adventure as wide as the earth? Can I lead the French by dreams?" The goal of the quest is *Le Salut* (Salvation), title of the third volume of the General's *Memoirs*.

> Then they burned Joan of Arc. And right off they thought that with her they were burning, and destroying forever, that marvelous flower whose seed seems to have been sown by Angels, that talent for honor which our race has made so transcendent that it almost

became a fourth theological virtue—oh our fathers! Oh our dead!

This from Bernanos' famous letter to "Dear Mr. Hitler" (!) in *Les Grands Cimetières sous la lune*. It was Wendell Wilkie, according to De Gaulle, who alleged that the General mistook himself for Joan of Arc; references to her are amazingly scarce in the *Memoirs*, but in *La France et son armée*, the General explained that the most remarkable feature of Joan's epic was that the blows she struck had the support of the population, that at Orleans it was the people's enthusiasm which contributed to the defeat of the enemy, that the presence of Joan before the St. -Honoré Gate aroused such intense feeling as to procure her entry to the capital. Here is where De Gaulle becomes Joan: he will subordinate strategy to mystical communion, either verbal or physical, with the people, the famous "bains de foule", leading to a parareligious exhortation:

> Come to us! you still warmed by the Christian flame which spreads the light of love and of fraternity through the valley of human travails, the valley which from century to century has kindled the spiritual inspiration of the nation. Social justice, national tradition, Christian flame, these three torches which illuminate French History in turn.

One has only to read Bernanos' own BBC speeches, or his unspoken but Ciceronian *Lettre aux Anglais* to recognize the same emphatic orchestration of a mystical and chivalric idea of France.

It may well be that De Gaulle and Bernanos owe their consanguinity to their mutual admiration of Charles Péguy; Bernanos did not, of course, have access to the General's *Memoirs*, he had to go by the broadcast speeches or broadsides. This makes his intuitive identification with his fellow exiled prophet the more extraordinary: it is through his words that the General appropriates the allegiance, even the *identity*, of the novelist. "General De Gaulle did not cheat," Bernanos writes in his first mention dated January 1942, Brazil. Because he was a novelist and a royalist, he maintains a real reticence toward De Gaulle through June 1943, trying to avoid any party politics; but with the third anniversary of the 18th of June, all restraint is swept aside in a journal entry entitled: "What do you want? There is France":

Frenchmen, we are being called on to forget our divisions; but when the job is completed we should end up by forgetting ourselves. Frenchmen, if we want to move together toward the future, it is imperative to choose in our past a rallying point. The History of France awaits you on the threshold of the 18th of June 1940; that is what I wanted to say. For History, this day is not Armistice Day; History doesn't give a damn about the Armistice, the Armistice is a large, worthless fact, useless for History, an enormous fetus, fat as a mountain. June 18, 1940 is the day when a predestined man, whether you chose him matters not—History presents him to you, has with a single word which cancelled defeat kept France in the war. Frenchmen, those who try to make you believe that this day and this man do not belong to all Frenchmen are wrong or are deceiving you. Join the mainstream of French History!

It is as the rebel, the leader by dreams that De Gaulle becomes a hero, *almost a literary hero,* in the Bernanosian universe: "A legend has formed around the event and the man. Be careful if you try to tamper with the event and the man"; do not heed the realists, they are the *tricheurs.* De Gaulle is the authentic voice who knows "what the world's expectations are."

Like the Romantic poet-seer, like Bernanos the novelist-prophet, De Gaulle's voice, on war-time radio and in the public arena, is oracular. Bernanos' collected newspaper articles of 1945-1948, *Frenchmen, if you knew* . . . restate the definition until it becomes self-definition of Bernanos *as* De Gaulle. "To speak in France's name, even if only once, is given to a very few predestined beings! General De Gaulle has spoken in France's name. We shall have to wait another ten years or ten centuries before, at another critical moment, the French spirit again finds expression in a single Frenchman." Always, like Bernanos himself, the General is the rejected savior alone in the purity of exile: "at Colombey, he will seem as lonely as in London. I say 'seem', because it is only the appearance of solitude: France continues and General De Gaulle with her." The enemies of both general and novelist are *les imbéciles,* the expedient politicians. When Malraux told a New York *Times* interviewer, John Hess, that De Gaulle called the 1969 referendum on regional reform because *he wanted to be beaten,* because *he sought ingratitude,* he articulated what Bernanos conveyed implicitly in his articles: that only rejected prophets have the privilege of limitless vituperation, of self-created existence in the Flesh made Word.

And so while De Gaulle dictated his memorialist's idea of France in the silence of Colombey in 1946, Bernanos spoke for him in a daring series of six *imaginary messages,* entitled *The General speaks to you.* In menacing tones worthy of Bossuet and with a choler more Bernanosian than 'Gaulliste', he denounces the betrayal of France by Frenchmen: "For five years now you've refused all risk . . . Imbeciles!" France is selling out to materialism, to statistics of prosperity: "You don't sacrifice the remaining nervous energy of a great people to fat, eunuchs are also fat." France must turn away from politics: France should not play politics, but make History. And the old Maurrassian distinction still haunts the General's persona (Bernanos' long flirtation with *L'Action Française* will be recalled): "Frenchmen, to save you it is not enough that I be the head of state, I must be at the head of France." For what France was, "a civilization, a gift of nature, a grace from God," is threatened by the inhumanity of modern technology embodied in the modern state itself: "State against nation. Technology against life." These words are among Bernanos' last.

How the author of these imaginary messages where he pretends to be De Gaulle would have judged the Fifth Republic we can only guess. How the General himself would have made the transition from the six projected chapters of *L'Effort* to the seventh, the evocation of the great figures of French History must also remain conjecture. Whether the praxis of *grandeur* betrayed a *certain idea of France,* in its insistence on modernization and technology, is a mystery for poets and critics to solve, and since I have been dealing with Bernanos and De Gaulle as poets of history not as historians, it seems appropriate to restate their fraternity of vision by citing Malraux, that *devotee of high destinies,* as De Gaulle called him. What Malraux says of De Gaulle must also be applied to Bernanos: "He had a profound relationship with the woodcutters of Colombey, but the woodcutters, you see, are the Middle Ages. For the general, the *people* was the people of the 12th century; it was not at all a belief in the superiority of money and things like that—which he despised—but it was men, the men of the forest and fields, and not the men of the factories. He never knew what a worker was, never, never."

From the mystique of De Gaulle as 'literary hero' in the reactionary quixotism of Bernanos, from shared dreams of the *pays réel,* we must return to the reality of History, to the meeting of the two dreamers some six month's after the novelist's return from Brazil. The very text of De Gaulle's telegram urging his admirer's return to France initiated a network of misunderstanding and disappointment: "Your place is here with us. Come back." In 1947, Bernanos was to characterize the message as written in the form of a semi-official order from a man he didn't know. But he was flattered nonetheless, as well as irritated; and he indicated by return wire that what with family, furniture, dogs, cats, goats and a parakeet, he would need a cargo ship to effect his return. Two months later, a naval officer arrived in the exile's farmyard in Brazil, saluted and proclaimed that he came from the General and that the boat was there. "I began to understand that with De Gaulle you didn't argue." But, as Luc Estang was to narrate it at the *Décade de Cerisy* devoted to Bernanos, these attentions led Bernanos to misread the intention of the telegram. He began to wonder whether De Gaulle wanted him in the Cabinet; he was embarrassed, after consulting extensively with friends as to which ministry was appropriate, when no offer was forthcoming, and a casual meeting or two with the General provided little consolation: "I began to ask myself why he wanted me to come back."

It is not clear whether Bernanos paid two visits to Colombey or whether we have two informally recollected narrations (by Luc Estang quoting Bernanos and by Bernanos himself) of a single formal meeting. I think the failure of communication was such that a second meeting seems an improbability. In any case, Bernanos was led to believe that De Gaulle wanted an extensive meeting, and he agreed. A lieutenant came to fetch him at 8:00 A. M., their destination, Colombey-les Deux-Eglises: "That struck me. I said to the lieutenant 'He needs two of them for himself, I have quite enough to do with one Church.' " Luc Estang quotes Bernanos upon his return from Colombey:

> He's something, that man. I arrived, we lunched. We didn't say much and then we went to the living room where aunt Yvonne was knitting [Mme De Gaulle]. I thought he was going to ask me questions. Non. He listened to me talking, and I talked, and from time to time he would say 'I understand,' and I continued talking and he kept saying 'I understand,' and suddenly it was time to get back in the car, and here I am.

In its collection of documents marking De Gaulle's death in November 1970, *L'Express* published a more poetic account, labelled enigmatically "Remarks gathered in 1947":

> We arrived for dinner in a typical country house. I really was intimidated. He was too. We drank an apéritif, then we lunched. It was deadly. He had nothing to say to me nor I to him. After coffee, it was so unbearable that I did what anyone would have done. I got up, went to the window, pulled back the curtain and looked at the garden. And I said: "It's raining." Then De Gaulle got up to join me, he pulled aside the rest of the curtain and he said: "Yes, it's raining."
>
> That's all. If we had a shared passion, and I think we did, it was an ineffable one. I understood that before he did.

Not long after this meeting Bernanos resumed his itinerant exile: Sisteron, Bandol, Tunisia. The meeting at Colombey must be seen as the strange, almost Pirandellian, encounter of a novelist with his persona. De Gaulle had become, in Bernanos' *Imaginary messages, The General speaks to you,* a *literary* character indispensable to the novelist's private mythology. But as autonomous *historical* characters, in the tradition of nostalgic Catholic Don Quixotes, De Gaulle and Bernanos did share a passion, a certain mystical idea of France that even reality could not destroy.

Chapter IV

The Catholic Novelist as Baptist: Flannery O'Connor

An epigraph is an author's apostolic blessing to his creation as it goes forth to meet the infidel. And when that epigraph becomes eponymous, it reveals itself an emblem of the meaning of that creation. The famous *regnum coelorum vim patitur, et violenti rapiunt illud* of Matthew XI, 12 has generally been considered one of the most polyvalent passages in the Gospels. "We cannot be sure of its meaning. If the context were certain, interpretation would be easier," says *The Interpreter's Bible.* The monks of Maredsous admit that it is a "passage énigmatique." The *King James Bible* translates "the kingdom of heaven suffereth violence, and the violent take it by force." The *Revised Standard Version* agrees, but in modernized terms: "the kingdom of heaven has suffered violence, and men of violence take it by force," with the alternative "has been coming violently." These are all restrictive rather than qualitative interpretations. Only the monks of Maredsous seem in harmony with Flannery O'Connor's epigraph. They write "le royaume des cieux est remporté de force et ce sont les violents qui le conquièrent." This is much more positive, even prescriptive, as indeed would seem to be the intent of Flannery O'Connor's interpretation: "the kingdom of heaven suffereth violence, and the violent bear it away." In other words, the kingdom of heaven does not suffer from violence, it authorizes it; and to the violent belongs the kingdom—they bear away the prize of salvation after the struggle.

There are two orders of baptism in the *Gospel according to Saint Matthew,* John the Baptist's and Christ's own, and in the narration the two coexist in parallel from III, 1 through XI, 13. John's repentance was a formula for violent exorcism: "every tree which bringeth not forth good fruit is hewn down, and cast into the fire"; his prophecy of Christ's order of baptism speaks of the Holy Ghost and of fire. But in the chapter from which Flannery O'Connor derived her epigraph, this prophecy was belied by Jesus himself: for His way is the new way of rest: "I am meek and lowly in heart, and ye shall find rest unto your souls. For my yoke is easy, and my burden is light." John's denunciation of the vipers' generation of Pharisees and Sadducees does indeed anticipate Christ's "Woe unto thee, Chorazin! woe unto thee, Bethsaida," but in Chapter 11 of Matthew we come to an historical transition from the intemperate old order of fire and action to the new code of patient instruction through parable and example. Jesus takes the measure of John and finds him wanting: "he that is least in the kingdom of heaven is greater than he. And from the days of John the Baptist until now the kingdom of heaven suffereth violence," etc.

This brief exegesis may help us to assess the violence of salvation in Flannery O'Connor's vision as well as her relationship to the violent thaumaturgical novelists I have described as "quixotic reactionaries." It is no accident that the Christian denomination of the South is 'Baptist' and that religious extremists in that region are 'fundamentalists.' for Flannery O'Connor sees the essential strategy of salvation as a return to the stormy principles of the prophet in the wilderness. We are not now ready for the kingdom of heaven to be taken by the suave yoke and lightened burden of Christ's love; *our* juncture of spiritual history is that of John the Baptist and of violent conquest of the kingdom (*A diebus autem Joannis Baptistae usque nunc*). "I'm as good, Mr. Motes, not believing in Jesus as many a one that does," the Pharisee landlady, Mrs. Flood, tells the hero of *Wise Blood*. Motes belongs to the violent order of hewing down the tree which does not bring forth good fruit and casting it in the fire. In the tradition of the desert fathers, he has mutilated himself by striking the mote or beam from his seeing eyes with quicklime, by filling his shoes with broken glass and stones, by wrapping three strands of barbed wire around his chest:

"It's easier to bleed than sweat, Mr. Motes," she said in the voice of High Sarcasm. "You must believe in Jesus or you wouldn't do these foolish things. You must have been lying to me when you named your fine church Church without Christ. I wouldn't be surprised if you weren't some kind of a agent of the pope or got some connection with something funny."

Like the prophet vagabond, the blind Hazel Motes ventures forth into the wilderness. Two policemen, summoned by Mrs. Flood, find him in a drainage ditch two days later. He dies in the police car after being clubbed, but in death Hazel marks the transition from the era of the Baptist to the era of Christ as he becomes a pinpoint of light in the darkness of the Pharisee's soul. The violence of the self-inflicted mutilations has yielded to the passivity of Christ the victim, when Mrs. Flood gazes into "the deep burned eye sockets . . . into the tunnel where it had disappeared" and toward that far away point of light.

Flannery O'Connor's obsession with the regression to a fundamentalist strategy of exorcism is, of course, most convincingly dramatized in *The Violent bear it away*, for Francis Marion Tarwater is John the Baptist reincarnate. One can say of him, as Jesus says of John in Matthew XI, 18: "For John came neither eating nor drinking, and they say He hath a devil." The oft-noted sun imagery in this novel is the very emblem of the Baptist's name day, the day of the summer solstice. Little wonder then that the devil proclaims "There's your sign," when the blinding brightness strikes the fountain as the holy idiot Bishop moves toward it: "Then the light, falling more gently, rested like a hand on the child's white hand. His face might have been a mirror where the sun had stopped to watch its reflection." The tonality struck by the epigraph finds echoes throughout the novel, making it an archetypal new version of Matthew's narration of John's mission. Like the Baptist, Tarwater (baptism is contained in his very name) comes from the wilderness to the city to baptize and to prophesy. He is an emissary of God, of someone who said he was his great-uncle but is referred to constantly as 'the old Man,' a spectral voice urging Tarwater to baptize a new Christ, the innocent child Bishop: "And the Lord, the old man said, has preserved the one child. . .from being corrupted by such parents. . .in the only possible way: the child was dim-witted." Late in the novel, Tarwater remembers his first meeting with Bishop:

> He had saved himself forever from the fate he had envisioned
> when, standing in the schoolteacher's hall and looking into the
> eyes of the dim-witted child, he had seen himself trudging off into
> the distance in the bleeding, stinking mad shadow of Jesus, lost
> forever to his own inclinations.

In that initial encounter, the mysterious presence of the patriarchal
God—the old man—had been transferred to Bishop: "he looked like
the old man grown backwards to the lowest form of innocence."
This 'son of God' is instinctively drawn to water, almost like Jesus
soliciting baptism from John (Matthew III, 13ff); twice he tempts
Tarwater by wandering into a fountain. Finally, heeding his demonic
voice and the signal from the sun, Tarwater resolves to drown the
boy, to murder God as he had thought to incinerate the great-uncle's
remains. But in the very act, meaning only to drown, he murmurs
the sacramental formula: "they were just some words that ran out
of my mouth and spilled in the water." The Pentecostal banner in
the slum tabernacle had borne the words *"Unless ye be born again ye
shall not have everlasting life."* Tarwater *will* be reborn into everlasting life as a reincarnation of Jesus, not of the Baptist. If he had
hoped to burn "the old man's fancies out of him," the fire in the
woods had been the fulfillment of John's prophecy of baptism
through fire. He had tried to murder, had instinctively baptized
Bishop into everlasting life. Now, however, returning to old Tarwater's woods he meets a new devil, "a pale, lean, old-looking
young man," who tempts him with tobacco and whiskey ("It's
better than the Bread of Life!" Tarwater proclaims drunkenly);
and following the perverted communion ceremony, the stranger
rapes him: "his delicate skin had acquired a faint pink as if he had
refreshed himself on blood." Tarwater raped becomes *a Christ-like
victim;* but he will be reborn as a prophet once more when he puts
fire to the woodland setting of the violation, as though to purify
himself and the world:

> His scorched eyes no longer looked hollow or as if they were
> meant only to guide him forward. They looked as if, touched with
> a coal like the lips of the prophet, they would never be used for
> ordinary sights again.

Flannery O'Connor compares Tarwater's progress homeward to
Moses' return to the promised land. If the devil's voice tempts

Tarwater once more, his answer is still fire, "the fire that had encircled Daniel, that had raised Elijah from the earth, that had spoken to Moses and would in the instant speak to him." Tarwater's final gesture is to pick up a handful of dirt from the simple grave the Negro Buford had made for the old man and to smear it on his forehead. The ashes of repentance become one with the earth of regeneration (compare my analysis of the ashes in *Vipers Tangle* in Chapter II, p. 40). The old man's command *"Go warn the children of God of the terrible spread of mercy"* is likened to seeds opening one at a time in his blood. Like John the Baptist, Tarwater had gone into the city as a prophet of violence; like Christ himself he will now go toward the "dark city, where the children of God lay sleeping," as a prophet of mercy.

That Mason Tarwater's violence was the necessary final station of the old order of John the Baptist is confirmed by the story of Bishop's biological father, the schoolteacher Rayber. Just before Bishop wanders to the fountain, Rayber cautions Tarwater:

> "The old man used to enrage me until I learned better. He wasn't worth my hate and he's not worth yours. He's only worth our pity . . . You want to avoid extremes. They are for violent people and you don't want . . . " he broke off abruptly as Bishop let loose his hand and galloped away.

This advocate of 'moderation' had himself been tempted to drown Bishop, but his nerve had failed: "You didn't have the guts," Tarwater taunts him. "He always told me you couldn't do nothing, couldn't act." At first glance, Rayber seems to be exactly what the critics have said, the lukewarm Pharisee. His father had been an insurance salesman who would sell you a policy against any contingency, including danger to the soul (see my remarks on Bernanos as the apostle of risk, p. 66). He called himself a "prophet of life insurance," and we all know what Catholic novelists think of "insurance" in the light of the Pascalian wager. With his interest in aptitude tests, his popular psychology magazine article analyzing the fanaticism of Old Tarwater, and his marriage to the "welfare woman," Rayber would join the ranks of countless caricatured intellectuals and believers in progress that populate the works of Bernanos. Rayber remembers the day he was informed of Bishop's condition and was told to be grateful his son's health at least was good. He had asked the classic question of the non-believer, of Ivan Karamazov: "How can I be grateful, when one—just one—is born with a heart outside?" *Grateful* takes on full etymological force here.

Yet Rayber *is* the father of the holy fool Bishop. He is more than a caricature of a Pharisee; his function in *The Violent bear it away* is to be a double, a mirror, of young Tarwater. *He* is a Tarwater who has rejected violence and by this abdication failed. As he looks at Tarwater, Rayber realizes "with an intense stab of joy that his nephew looked enough like him to be his son." Like Tarwater, Rayber had been borne away by the 'old man,' kidnapped literally, and baptized. For a time he had been an extreme fundamentalist himself. He seems to have become disillusioned, but we learn that he has merely repressed or distorted his vocation:

> The affliction was in the family. It lay hidden in the line of blood that touched them, flowing from some ancient source; some desert prophet or polesitter, until its power unabated, it appeared in the old man and him and, he surmised, in the boy . . . . He had kept it from gaining control over him by what amounted to a rigid ascetic discipline . . . . He slept in a narrow iron bed, worked sitting in a straight-backed chair, ate frugally, spoke little . . . He knew that he was the stuff of which fanatics and madmen are made.

As he walks, Christlike, barefoot through the streets of the city in pursuit of Tarwater, a chorus of small boys sings: "Hi yo, silverware, Tonto's lost his underwear!" Tarwater is a "Lone Ranger," and as his companion with the name of Madman (Tonto) Rayber finds him at a pentecostal meeting. A child is preaching *(revelasti ea parvulis,* Matthew, XI, 25): "The Word of God is a burning Word, to burn you clean." With the taste of his own childhood on his tongue "like a bitter wafer", Rayber looks in through the window, an outsider. He had made his barefoot calvary, only to receive from a child the revelation of his fall:

> "Listen you people," she shrieked, "I see a damned soul before my eye! I see a dead man Jesus hasn't raised. His head is in the window, but his ear is deaf to the Holy Word!"

Rayber's only escape is to turn off his hearing-aid, to acknowledge his deafness. He had lost his hearing when he had gone to the old man to reclaim his kidnapped nephew and been shot at. Rayber had no gun with which to counterattack; he once again rejected violence, and his hearing-aid represents the barrier modern scientific man has erected against the violent, gun-shot sound of salvation. Despite his vocation for violence and blasphemy, those two essential bypaths to salvation (Rayber sprinkles water over his nephew's bottom, remarking "Now Jesus has a claim on both ends,") Rayber has indeed become a 'moderate' and a realist. When Tarwater stops before a bakery window containing a single loaf of bread, the schoolteacher's only thought is "If he had eaten his dinner, he wouldn't be happy." We recall Rayber's father's words at his son's baptism: "One bath more or less won't hurt the bugger." And of course, Flannery O'Connor's own preface to *Wise Blood:* "That belief in Christ is to some a matter of life and death has been a stumbling block for readers who would prefer to think it a matter of no great consequence." The schoolteacher would be one of those readers: he is a potential John the Baptist who has turned a deaf ear to the *vocatus* of baptism. "He's full of nothing," the old man had said of his nephew. After Bishop's death, Rayber collapses upon the realization that there would be no pain, no hurt, no feeling. His emptiness is the fulfillment of his own prophecy for Tarwater: "This one is going to be brought up to live in the real world . . . . He's going to be his own saviour. He's going to be free."

Flannery O'Connor's comments on violence in her own work have been oft quoted, much discussed, but only partially understood. In the light of my reading of the epigraph to *The Violent bear it away* as the culmination of the Johannine mission before the advent of the gentle yoke of Jesus, I believe that her mission as a writer stands more clearly revealed in the Catholic tradition of quixotic romantic reactionaries. She wrote in "The Fiction Writer & his Country" (in *Mystery and Manners*):

> The novelist with Christian concerns will find in modern life distortions which are repugnant to him, and his problem will be to make these appear as distortions to an audience which is used to seeing them as natural; and he may well be forced to take ever more

violent means to get his vision across to this hostile audience. When you can assume that your audience holds the same beliefs you do, you can relax a little and use more normal means of talking to it; when you have to assume that it does not, then you have to make your vision apparent by shock—*to the hard of hearing you shout, and for the almost-blind you draw large and startling figures* (italics mine).

The analogy immediately brings to mind the deaf schoolteacher Rayber and the mote in the eye of the hero of *Wise Blood*. In her introductory remarks to a reading of *A Good Man is Hard to Find* at Hollins College, the author elaborates on this, after citing Baudelaire's aphorism that the devil's greatest ruse is to convince us that he does not exist:

> We hear many complaints about the prevalence of violence in modern fiction, and it is always assumed that this violence is a bad thing and meant to be an end in itself. With the serious writer, violence is never an end in itself. It is the *extreme situation* that best reveals what we are essentially, and I believe these are times when writers are more interested in what we are essentially than in the tenor of our daily lives. Violence is a force which can be used for good or evil, and *among other things taken by it is the kingdom of heaven* (italics mine). But regardless of what can be taken by it, the man in the violent situation reveals those qualities least dispensable in his personality, those qualities which are all he will have to take into eternity with him.

If I read these important lines correctly, they mean that the author's relation to her work is identical to John the Baptist's incendiary assault on the kingdom of heaven. Her fiction marks the culmination of John's way ("the last of the Old Testament prophets," the Jerusalem Bible calls him) in anticipation of the hoped for eventual transition to the way of Jesus, the way of the victim. Flannery O'Connor and the prophet in the wilderness both want to hew down the unfruitful tree and cast it into the fire. Moreover, the author's relation to her material must be likened to the reaction of old Tarwater and his nephew to the "normal" lives of the lukewarm. *What the novelist does by means of violent plots and language, the characters do in their actions.* "I am more and more impressed with the amount of Catholicism that fundamentalist Protestants have been able to retain. Theologically, our differences are on the nature of the Church, not on the nature of God or our obligations to Him." This letter from Miss O'Connor to Sister Mariella Gable seems almost a re-working of Christ's assessment of John's mission in Matthew XI. Flannery O'Connor *may have been a Roman Catholic, but she is, quite literally, a Baptist.*

In contrast to John's reliance on threats of direct action and punishment, Christ's method in Matthew XI is instruction through parables, exemplary maxims or miracles. Here, too, O'Connor reveals herself a Baptist. Tarwater said, after drowning Bishop: "There are them that can act and them that can't, and them that are hungry and them that ain't. That's all. I can act. And I ain't hungry." The intellectual Rayber "couldn't do nothing, couldn't act," his nephew tells him after he admitted his failure of nerve with Bishop. Rayber believes in "questions that meant more than one thing, planting traps around the house watching him fall into them." One could, of course, prepare a statistical study of the number of murders, suicides, rapes and insults in O'Connor's work (as I have done with Bernanos in Chapter III) to prove her commitment to violent action as a means of dispelling the cloud of non-being of the Pharisees. "I'll make it happen. I can act," Tarwater had said to a traveling salesman. But O'Connor's strategy is more complex. What in parable had been figurative, even ambiguous, she removes from the realm of pure language: *she makes it happen.* This is especially true of her prophet figures' messages and the hortatory signs of the fundamentalists. *Woe to the Blasphemer and Whoremonger. Will Hell Swallow You Up?* Hazel Motes reads on a roadside sign. These words become action: he goes to the whore Leora Watts; he becomes a preacher of blasphemy in the *Church without Christ.* If his very name contains the figurative "mote" in the eye (*vide* Matthew, VII, 3-5), Hazel Motes makes his blindness total and literal. Unlike the false blindman, Asa Hawks, the Evangelist whose nerve failed at the last moment (the same words were applied to Rayber and the drowning), Motes' blindness allows him to shut out the false light of Lucifer and to see the purest light. If the epigraph from Matthew tells us "that the violent bear it away," this too becomes direct action: Old Tarwater kidnaps both Rayber and Francis Marion to baptize them. When an evangelist echoes Christ's words that "Wisdom comes out of the mouth of babes," a child commences to preach. Her own words in that sermon also move from the figurative to literal enactment. The man whose "head is in the window but his ear is deaf to the Holy Word" is actually looking through the window and shuts off his hearing-aid. The child's message to Tarwater was: "The Word of God is a burning Word, to burn you clean." He turns the Word to flame by setting fire to the woods.

The same pattern is maintained in the most violent of the short stories. Mrs. Greenleaf exorcises evil by clipping newspaper stories of rapes, divorces and plane crashes, burying the documents in holes in the woods (*Greenleaf* in *Everything that rises must converge*). The Pharisee Mrs. May, who thought the word "Jesus" should be kept inside the church building like other words inside the bedroom," comes upon the prayer healer writhing on the ground covering her clippings, and groaning: "Jesus! Jesus! Stab me in the heart!" For Mrs. May (her very name indicates latent potential), "the sound was so piercing that she felt as if some violent unleashed force had broken out of the ground and was charging toward her." At the end of the story, the bull which had strayed from the Greenleaf farm sinks his horn into her heart "like a tormented lover," while his victim takes on the look "of a person whose sight has been suddenly restored but who finds the light unbearable." The words of the prayer have become action. In one of O'Connor's very finest stories, *The Lame Shall Enter First* (a reworking of Tarwater's story really), Norton longs for his dead mother. When the fundamentalist Rufus Johnson, another one of those Dostoevskian holy criminals, tells the boy that his mother is "on high" because she believed in Jesus and you have to be dead to get there, Norton begins looking for her through a telescope. His social worker father, Mr. Sheppard, had taught him about space travel; now Norton launches his flight into space by hanging himself. The fraudulent "good shepherd" ("He thinks he's Jesus Christ," the ungrateful Rufus says) tells the fundamentalist who is reading the Bible at the dinner table that he is too intelligent to believe literally in the Word; whereupon Johnson (the son of John, after all) rips out a page and swallows it whole! The whorish Sarah Ham (see my earlier remarks on the dangers of allegorical names for Catholic novelists, p. 39), in *The Comforts of Home*, laughingly asks Thomas as he drives recklessly: "Jesus, where's the fire?" The fire is in his loins, in his revolver, and ultimately in hell, as he shoots his mother who had thrown herself in front of his intended victim, Sarah:

> Thomas fired. The blast was like a sound meant to bring an end to evil in the world. Thomas heard it as a sound that would shatter the laughter of sluts until all shrieks were stilled and nothing was left to disturb the peace of perfect order.

The police mistakenly think that he plotted with the girl to kill the mother; and yet perhaps they were right: the firing of the gun *was* a sexual act, expressing oedipal love and hate. That literal enactment of the answer to the question "Where's the fire?" becomes figurative or symbolic once more. The fire becomes the image of the Hell a doubting Thomas must forever more inhabit.

This movement back from the literal to the symbolic marks a cadence leading to harmonic resolution in Flannery O'Connor's violent world of action (of figurative language made literal by enactment). As I have shown in the example of Mauriac and the supernatural (Chapter II, p. 40), a prosaic word or gesture suddenly flows back into the great mainstream of consecrated Christian symbolism. Hazel Motes' words to the truckdriver "Take your hand off me. I'm reading the sign" becomes the *noli mi tangere* of Jesus, and "the sign" is that of the cross. "I'm Father Finn—from Purgatory," a hearty priest announces to identify himself and his home parish. Mrs. May's casual and empty expletive "I thank God for that!" is answered by Mr. Greenleaf's "I thank Gawd for ever-thang." When Tarwater smears dirt from his great-uncle's grave on his forehead, he is reenacting a symbolic gesture (see Mauriac's *Vipers' Tangle*, my Chapter II, p. 40) that has marked Ash Wednesday penitents since the founding of the Church.

The essential violence of salvation in the works of Flannery O'Connor must, however, be viewed as a combination of these techniques: a movement from the figurative to the literal and then back to a renewed and heightened figuration in a Christological pattern. This is, of course, the very progression of poetry, which takes the words of the tribe, originally liturgical and magically incantatory, concretizes them and finally reendows them with symbolic power. "The only way to the truth is through blasphemy," Hazel Motes preaches; familiar words, as we have seen, to readers of Elisabeth Langgässer and Graham Greene, as well as to disciples of Baudelaire and De Maistre, notably Barbey d'Aurevilly and Bernanos. Blasphemy began as a satanic *non serviam* of negative faith, then becomes meaningless expletive or absent faith. "Jesus, Jesus." Motes says in panic to a sleeping-car porter closing the curtain of his berth around him. "Jesus been a long time gone," the porter answers in "a sour and triumphant voice." An empty oath is abruptly made literal and then takes on a renewed symbolic or figurative power. The most striking example, though countless others could be adduced, can be found in the rightly admired used-car lot scene in *Wise Blood*. The young apprentice car-salesman's relentless swearing is likened to a hacking cough. To Motes' query on a car "How much is it?" he answers vacuously "Jesus on the cross. Christ nailed." "Why don't he shut up," Motes mutters angrily. For Hazel Motes, blasphemy is a serious business, not a verbal tic, and is the central article of negative faith in his Church without Christ. But the contradiction of his naive belief in swearing as a means of denying Jesus soon becomes apparent. During one of his prosletyzing homilies to a young garage attendant, he explains his new awareness "that you couldn't even believe in that blasphemy because then you were believing in something to blaspheme" (Ivan Karamazov's devil is lurking in the shadows here.). As Motes says this, he begins to act out his own spiritual discovery, cursing "in a quiet intense way but with such conviction that the boy paused from his work to listen." The very purchase of the run-down old Essex car was intended as an act of blasphemy: "nobody with a good car needs to be justified." Instead, the car leads Motes toward the stations of redemption. As he drives from the lot onto the highway lined with fundamentalist signs, he reads: *"Woe to the Blasphemer and Whoremonger! Will Hell Swallow You Up?"* And in smaller letters, at the bottom of the sign: "Jesus Saves."

For Flannery O'Connor, the Word always leads to the Act, and this, not what one benighted regionalist critic has called "gratuitous gothic," is the origin and justification for her obsession with violence. When Mrs. Turpin hears herself assaulted by an hysterical Wellesley student named Mary Grace with the words: "Go back to hell where you came from, you old wart hog," she goes to the hog-pen and receives confirmation of the *Revelation* (the name of the story). In *The Fiction Writer & His Country,* we read: "The anguish that most of us have observed for some time now has been caused not by the fact that the South is alienated from the rest of the country, but by the fact that it is not alienated enough, that every day we are getting more and more like the rest of the country, that we are being forced out not only of our many sins, but of our few virtues." Rufus Johnson's literal belief in hell, in the incontrovertible teratology of Satan's world is manifested physically in his monstrously swollen foot. The wilfully good Mr. Sheppard, with his modern theories of social rehabilitation, tries to camouflage that physical incarnation of evil with a specially therapeutic shoe. In so doing, he seeks to make the extreme into something moderate. Flannery O'Connor seeks through violence to sharpen the barrier between herself and "the rest of the country." She leads away from intention and back to action. Melodrama is by definition bloody, but there is in blood both redemption and wisdom. One may be disgusted by blood, one may be morbidly attracted, one cannot remain neutral, impassive and lukewarm.

Chapter V

Irreverence and Sanctity: Heinrich Böll

Heinrich Böll often lets his better nature get the worst of him. Many of the elements in his early work now seem rather sentimental (which is one reason his late works have become increasingly sardonic). The lonely figure of the *Landser,* the ordinary soldier, a mere pawn overwhelmed by events on the front and stumbling uncomprehendingly and without protest toward an absurd, useless, and inevitable death; the omnipresent railway stations through which people pass on their way to the front or on their return to obliterated homes, stations where no one ever is met; the consistent use of flashback techniques which evoke a wistful nostalgia for an orderly, though already hypocritical, world *before* the war; internal monologues by the main characters, consecutive but rarely converging, thus heightening our awareness that the essential human condition is solitary introspection, not solidarity; and everywhere the orphans and victimized children. Joining with these better impulses is a fine sense of the ridiculous: the music-loving, concentration camp commander, *Obersturmführer* Filskeit, who grants a stay of execution to those prisoners who can enrich the camp choir by singing on pitch, and provisionally ignores the principles of his own prize-winning monograph on "the relationship between race and choir." Böll's comment on Dickens' sense of humor seems a perfect self-definition: Dickens' eye was always a little moist, and the Latin word for moisture is *Humor.*"

Back in the 1950's, when Böll's first novels and tales appeared in English some five years or so after their publication in German, his apparent sentimentality constituted a good measure of his attraction. We were relieved, I suppose that Geroge Steiner, in his role as Cassandra of the death of German literary language, was being undercut by a talent as impressive as Böll's, though one wondered in those dynamic days of German economic recovery whether the writers in their Volkswagens had forgotten the war and the concentration camps as quickly as the industrialists in their Mercedes. Günter Grass had not yet been translated, and despite reports on the literary scene in Europe in various periodicals, we were pretty ignorant of the new voices. Was there literary material in the horror, or merely superlative statistics for sociologists? Böll's early works provided a welcome tentative answer. His melody was pure; his mode understatement; his style apparently sparse, almost factual. He was attractive too because he was a Catholic who, despite the war, did not seem obsessed with the Apocalypse in the way that makes Elisabeth Langgässer's work so excessive. Böll was compassionate rather than visionary, though he was perhaps overly fond of his own characters and, implicitly, a bit self-indulgent; he had not yet shaken off that Rhineland sweetness which was later to annoy him so.

Like Flannery O'Connor, Heinrich Böll has a keen sense of the symbolic power of emblematic epigraphs and quotations in works depicting a disorderly world. *Und sagte kein einziges Wort (And he didn't say a word)*, his 1953 novel attacking religious hypocrisy, has a title which communicates the essence of his Christian vision: "He never said a mumblin' word," sings a Negro. The title is simply a German translation of the refrain from the spiritual (mistranslated back into English as "Acquainted with the Night" by R. Graves). "They nailed Him to the Cross, and He never said a word" Christ is the victim, He is overwhelmed by hostile forces, He does not protest His fate, He cannot even understand it— the cry of *"Lamma, Lamma, Sabachthani"* implies a metaphysic beyond the concept of Christ found in the simple spiritual. For the Böll of the novels and stories of the early 1950's, the victims, whether they be foot-soldiers or civilians, are "Christ"; and the executioners are the powerful of the earth, the officers, the industrialists, the Pharisees. As with Dostoevsky (and Böll's *The Clown* has much of the Dostoevskian in it), one can measure the saintliness of a character by the extent of his silences. The hangmen are articulate; Christ "never said a mumblin' word."

This pattern is made amply clear in the brilliant story, *Murke's Collected Silences,* first published in the *Frankfurter Hefte* in 1955. Murke, a *cum laude* graduate in psychology, works in the ultramodern Broadcasting House, where his existential morning prayer consists of riding through the locks of the paternoster lift, "open carriages carried on a conveyor belt, like beads on a rosary, . . . so that passengers could step on and off at any floor." Murke's pressing assignment in the Cultural Department is to reedit two talks on *The Nature of Art* by the great Professor Bur-Malottke, who had converted to Catholicism during the religious fervor of the guilt-ridden year of 1945, but who had 'deconverted' suddenly. In the two talks, "God" occurs twenty-seven times, and it is the Professor's intention to cut "god" out of the tapes and to replace Him with "the higher Being Whom we revere." That Murke, despite his degree in psychology, is the only Christian in the story, becomes apparent not only in the antipathy he feels toward Bur-Malottke, the go-getting opportunist caricatured in so many of Böll's works, but in two symbolic passages.

From his mother, Murke had received a tawdry, highly-colored print of the Sacred Heart with the words "I prayed for you at St. James Church." Instead of throwing out that sentimental card, he decides, in irritation at the "impressive rugs, the impressive corridors, the impressive furniture, and the pictures in excellent taste," to establish the Sacred Heart in the impeccable surroundings of Broadcasting House by sticking the print on the office door of the Assistant Drama Producer: "Thank God, now there's at least one corny picture in this place." The second passage involves Murke's extraordinary hobby. Against all network regulations, he collects leftover snips of tape: "When I have to cut tapes, in the places where the speakers sometimes pause for a moment—or sigh, or take a breath, or there is absolute silence—I don't throw that away. I collect it. Incidentally, there wasn't a single second of silence in Bur-Malottke's tapes." And in the evenings he splices the silences together and plays them to himself; "I have only three minutes so far—but then people aren't silent very often."

A perverse kind of deus ex machina brings the two strains together. The Assistant Drama Producer decides to revise an edifying radio play about an atheist who taunts God with questions and is answered only by silence. Twelve of Bur-Malottke's excised "God's" will replace the silences. "You really are a godsend," the Assistant Producer says to the technician who offers the snippets from Murke's tin collection box. And Murke now will be able to add almost a full minute of silence to his nightly tape-recorded prayers. The intimation here is that a real God is in those silences (compare my remarks on the supernatural in Chapter II, p. 27); the rest is sham. But the reader wonders whether that tawdry card with its inscription, "I prayed for you at St. James Church", did not also have some mystical effect on the producer, causing him mysteriously to revise his radio play.

"One must pray in order to console God," the Jewess Ilona in *Adam, Where Art Thou (Adam, wo warst du?)* had told the taciturn foot soldier Feinhals. One of Böll's more attractive traits as a Catholic novelist is that he finds Christ more often than not among the *non*-Christians and the unbelievers. It is Ilona who auditions for the concentration camp choir with the All-Saints Litany and who instead of appealing to the music-loving commandant with her angelic voice arouses in him such a sexual paroxysm of raging impotence and guilt that he shoots her. Pilate has done his job again. But Ilona's words live on in the former architect who had kissed her once before returning to the front. One must pray to console God for the faces and sermons of "His" priests, Feinhals thinks shortly before his pathetic death at the very doorstep of his home.

Among the most important currents in Böll's work, and one which links it to so many of the Catholic novelists I have been considering here, is his relentless caricaturing of the Pharisee. Truly, God needs consoling when faced with some of the faithful in *Acquainted with the Night (Und sagte kein einziges Wort)*. Mrs. Franke, a powerful force in diocesan intrigues, pronounces the word "money" with a tenderness which appalls, using just the intonation with which others might pronounce "life, love, death or God." Her work in the parish amounts to little more than trading "in the most precious of all commodities, in God." Even her domestic chores become reflections of her religiosity; she counts her preserve jars "as if she were gently chanting the cadences of some secret liturgy." In contrast, Böll presents us with two of his most touching characters, Fred and Kate, who would doubtless be castigated as sinners by a Mrs. Franke. Fred, whose father was an ex-priest, has left Kate out of self-hatred and now sleeps in the railway station, drinking heavily but sending what little money he has to his impoverished wife. They meet as guilt-ridden "lovers" in a sordid hotel room: "It is terrible to love and to be married."

As a social document, *Acquainted with the Night* might be read as a protest against poverty amid prosperity, or even as a treatise on the consequences of the postwar housing shortage. But it is, above all, a religious novel. Fred and Kate are among those who are crucified in silence. It is she who hears the Negro singing his plaintive spiritual. When Kate finally summons up enough nerve to go to a confessional, she sees the priest watching the clock and in anger protests against "the clergy who lived in great houses and had faces like advertisements for complexion cream." Through Fred's eyes, we see the hypocrisy of the postwar religious revival. Even a druggists' convention requires ecclesiastical collaboration. Amid signs proclaiming "Trust your Druggist" and balloons advertising toothpaste (one company actually drops tubes of dentrifice on the crowd—the new manna from heaven!) the clergy march with the bishop, apparently falling into an instinctive goosestep, heading the procession. But despite the venality, or perhaps because of it, the Host remains pristine, and Fred cannot resist kneeling and crossing himself: "For a moment I had the feeling of being a hypocrite until it came to my mind that God was not to blame for the inadequacies of His servants and that it was no hypocrisy to kneel before Him."

Unlike so many Catholic novelists I have been considering in this book (Bernanos, Julien Green, Langgässer, Graham Greene), Böll is refreshingly free from dualism. For him, the way to God does not necessarily lead first to Satan. Nor, however, does it lead to conventional orthodoxy. Fred Bogner is a true Christian; he sees through cant and he understands the true mystical impulse. He sympathizes with a priest who has become unpopular (achieving only a Delta-plus on his evaluation card) because his sermons were not sentimental enough for his parishoners' operetta tastes in religion. He recognizes in a strange vision of a holy family the sincerity of a pretty girl whose idiot brother, while frightened of life, is transformed by the singing of the monks.

That Fred's naive and instinctive mysticism is for him an ideal can be seen in the conclusion of an early Böll story, "Candles for Marie" (1950). Electricity has made candles obsolete, and an apparently callous candle manufacturer tries unsuccessfully to dispose of his now useless merchandise to a wholesaler in religious goods. Having missed his train one day, he follows a young couple into a church, tries to pray, confesses himself, and finally converts his very merchandise into prayer by lighting all the candles from his suitcase at the altar. "My heart felt happier than it ever had before," he is able to say at last.

In his *Letter to a Young Catholic*, Böll directly attacks the Church for its preoccupation with such superficial questions as determining what kinds of print and paper are most suitable for army prayerbooks. He cautions a prospective draftee against the new "gym-teacher's theology." Elsewhere, he warns writers against winking knowingly at their public. Almost all of his works with a postwar setting contribute to the current of anti-Pharisee humor initiated by *Acquainted with the Night*. (Böll himself succumbs occasionally to the Catholic in-jokes he derided in his memorable, virtually untranslatable phrase as *das Konfekt der Eingeweihten*—the candy of the confirmed.) Bertha, in the story "Like a Bad Dream," had learned from the nuns at boarding school that her husband should wear a dark jacket and conservative tie to consummate an important business deal. Did the nuns also teach her to know instinctively that her husband would have to offer a large bribe to win the contract, or that the best way to lure a colleague into an adjoining room to talk business was to suggest that he might be interested in seeing an eighteenth century crucifix hanging in that room. And yet it is she who in reaction to her husband's expletive, "Christ, it means 20,000 marks to me," answers: "One should never mention Christ's name in connection with money." Forceful and indignant when a man named Fink confesses his adultery with a married housewife, the priest in "The Adventure" changes his tone upon hearing that the houses which Fink sells are not quite they way they look in the catalogue. "The priest could not suppress an 'Aha'. He said: 'We must be honest about that too, although . . . ' he groped for words, 'although it seems impossible. But it is a lie to sell something of whose value one is not convinced.' " Those are double-edged words indeed with which to conclude the priest's admonition. Fink is weary and unable to pray until through half-closed, sleepy lids he sees a symbol of naive faith, the silhouette of a small old woman outlined in gigantic detail on the wall of the center nave: "a childlike nose and the tired slackness of her lips moving silently: a fleeting memorial, towering above the truncated plaster figures and seeming to grow out beyond the edge of the book."

Another key epigraph illuminating Böll's novelistic vision also serves as title to one of his earliest efforts, *Adam, Where Art Thou?* It is taken from the 1940 *Tag- und Nachtbücher (Diaries and Night-Thoughts)* of Theodore Häcker, and reads in full as follows: "A world catastrophe can be of great service. It can also serve as an alibi before God. 'Adam, where wert thou?' 'I was in the world war.'" For Germans of Böll's generation, the war was (as we have seen in Chapter I) the central existential event separating the few who retained their integrity from the many who gave in to "bad faith." Böll himself served on several fronts and was wounded in action; he will clearly not be one of those Romantics who glory in their fictitious role in an imaginary German Resistance. Nor will he offer breast-beating novels of remorse to assuage the conscience of his complacent compatriots. He accepts the incontrovertible necessity of service in the Wehrmacht, but asks implicitly: "What *kind* of soldier?" And he has far less sympathy for those on the home front making money than for the *Landser* shooting blindly at a faceless enemy. It would appear that in his works with a war setting, Böll often takes at face value the epigraph's ironic use of catastrophe as an alibi before God, but that were he to apply this epigraph to more recent works, *Billiards at Half-Past Nine* and *The Clown*, he would emphasize the irony.

He quotes as a second epigraph to *Adam, Where Art Thou?* Saint-Exupéry's locus classicus that war is a disease exactly like typhoid. Yet Böll, curiously enough, does not take very seriously, at least in his early works, his role as diagnostician. He neither describes the causes of infection nor offers prescriptions for a cure or preventive medicine. Though most of the Landser we meet in *The Train was on time (Der Zug war pünktlich,* 1940) and Adam are Catholic by birth, Böll never burdens his war novels with the recondite reli-

gious symbolism which I criticized in Mauriac's *The Lamb* or Langgässer's *The Indelible Seal* (in my Chapter II). Retrospectively, however, we can feel that the image of the crucifixion conveyed in the
words of the Negro spiritual would apply to his vision of the war:

> A crowd of infantry men and pioneers who seemed very tired
> were squatting near a barn and many of them lay on the ground
> smoking. Then they came to a town and on leaving it the man in
> the lookout heard shots for the first time. A heavy battery was firing
> from the right of the road. Huge barrels pointed steeply into the air,
> black against the dark blue sky. Blood-red fire spurted from the
> muzzles and cast a soft red reflection on the wall of a barn. The man
> ducked: he had never heard any shooting before and now he was
> frightened. He suffered from ulcers, very serious ulcers.

In this passage, the author seems objective and neutral, writing in
accordance with the esthetic of the now famous "new matter-of-
factness' (*neue Sachlichkeit*). The colors are exploited mainly for
chromatic contrast (black, then dark blue, then blood-red to soft
red), but they also mirror human emotions, although this is never
made explicit by any direct links between characters and colors.
(One might say that the progression of colors corresponds to the soldier's reactions to gunfire which run from apathy to fear to appre-
hensive resignation.) The plastic contours offer yet another contrast: the squatting men, the angular projections of the steeply
pointing barrels, the blurred outlines of a color reflected on the wall
of a barn. Despite the appearance of objectivity, this passage from
Adam, Where Art Thou? represents what I consider the sentimentality of Böll's war narratives. He tells us simply enough that the
lookout had never heard shots before, that he ducked and was
frightened. This description nonetheless creates a bond of sympathy
between reader and character, a bond heightened by the revelation,
still factual in tone, that the lookout had ulcers, very serious ulcers.
From the crowd of soldiers squatting and smoking, a detail which
leaves us emotionally indifferent, we move to the individual, a nervous worrier who is inexperienced, frightened, and tormented with
ulcers. Here is another victim about to be 'crucified' by the hostile,
faceless force of "heavy batteries," "huge barrels," "blood-red fire."

The lookout somehow seems terribly small; he does not protest, he only worries.

The plot of *Adam . . .* is typical of those found in Böll through *Billiards at Half-Past Nine,* in that fragments of different lives are narrated sequentially, brought together in momentary convergence, then dispersed again: solitude is the human predicament. Despite the large cast of characters in a very short book, the plot is basically simple, alternating between portraits and descriptions of soldiers *en situation.* Böll's double postulation of caricature and sentimental compassion is everywhere apparent. Thus, we have the Nazi Dr. Greck, a violent anti-Semite, contrasted with the helpless architect Feinhals and the Jewess Ilona: "You're like wolves that at any moment can begin to love," she says of the foot soldier. Too often, it seems to me, Böll structures his plot to evoke the maximum of pathos: the battle casualty, Captain Bauer, whose wife after many miscarriages got cancer, mysteriously whispers "Bjejogorsche" every fifty seconds, recalling Kurtz's repetition of "the horror . . ."; the innkeeper Kinck, ordered to procure a case of Tokay wine, is shot by a sniper while protecting his suitcase filled with the precious bottles; and when Feinhals has paid his visit of condolence to Finck's family in the neighboring village of Weidesheim and is in sight of his own home, he is struck down by a shell. The white tablecloth that his family has hung on the outside of their house to signify their surrender falls on Feinhals: a final shroud of purity, another silent death, another sentimental Böll *coup de théâtre.*

II

"I had always wanted to write, I tried my hand at it early, but it was only later that I found the right words," Böll wrote in a bibliographical essay in 1958. His recent novels recreate even more dramatically the tension between "irreverence and sanctity," particularly in *Billiards at Half-Past Nine* (1959) and *The Clown* (1963), until in *Group Portrait with Lady* (*Gruppenbild mit Dame,* 1971) the always hovering satirical bent takes over from the spiritual. I shall examine only those that are still in the Catholic tradition, namely

Billiards . . . and *The Clown;* they are among his noblest and most original creations.

The central event in *Billiards* is the eightieth birthday celebration of Heinrich Faehmel, the patriarch of a family now in its third generation in Bonn. Such an event is always a time for memories and self-appraisal, and this novel exists in the present through dialogue and in many fragments of the past through a complex network of internal monologues and leitmotifs owing more to Virginia Woolf and to *le nouveau roman* than to Faulkner or Joyce. The point of view in the novel is constantly shifting, often without real justification, and since the fête brings together all living members of this once large family, as well as coincidentally some outsiders who once played important roles in their lives, almost everyone is given extensive internal monologues. One of the failings of this perhaps too self-consciously complicated book is that these many monologues are not sufficiently individualized for the reader to grasp that the point of view (there are no real transitions) has once again changed. Be that as it may, what Böll clearly intends is for this family and its acquaintances to represent Germany, and for the constant summoning up of the past to afford an opportunity for measuring several generations of German spiritual and political history. The verdict, of course, is "weighed and found wanting."

The novel spans fifty-one years, from September 30, 1907, when Heinrich Faehmel successfully enters the architectural competition for the Benedictine Abbey of St. Anthony, to September 6, 1958, his birthday, at a time when the Abbey has been rebuilt after being destroyed during the war. On the eighty-year-old birthday child's cake sits a replica of the Abbey in frosting!) The Abbey itself represents Germany's attempt to hold on to a traditional, agrarian past, that romantic nostalgia which we have seen in so many Catholic novelists. Faehmel won first prize with his design:

> In the foreground, the hamlet of Stehlinger's Grotto, with grazing
> cows, a freshly dug potato field . . . And then, in powerful basilican
> style, the Abbey itself, which I'd boldly modeled after the Roman-
> esque cathedrals, with the cloister low, severe and somber, cells,
> refectory and library, the figure of St. Anthony in the center of the

cloister garth. Set off against the cloister the big quadrangle of farm buildings, granaries, barns, coach houses, own grist mill with bakery, a pretty residence for the steward, whose job was also to take care of the visitors on pilgrimage. And there, under high trees, simple tables and chairs at which to eat a meal, with dry wine, cider or beer, before setting out on the journey back . . . . Bread for his religious and for the poor, from grain harvested in his own fields. Yes, there, as an afterthought the young architect had added a little room for the beggars . . .

For the readers of Böll's *Irish Diaries (Irisches Tagebuch,* 1957), the vision is the familiar one of a pre-industrial world where poverty is still sacred, where man has been alienated neither from his soil nor from his God. But Böll is also less romantic than those I have labeled "quixotic reactionaries" in my first chapter. Unlike Bernanos and Waugh, say, who clung romantically to their storybook notion of the Middle Ages, Böll recognizes that beautiful as the life represented by the Abbey may be, it offers mere escape into the past, not an excuse for abdication of religious and social responsibility. Father Faehmel looks at his World War I bonds, his two medals, and his old banknotes, and realizes, too late, that his life was a failure. He had watched the "Higher Power" coming in, he had acquiesced in the war, had designed barracks, fortifications, and military hospitals. Only his wife Johanna had dared to blaspheme, had cried "That fool of a Kaiser!" Father Faehmel had agreed with her, but had refused to take a stand, saying instead to excuse her revolt that she was pregnant and had lost two brothers on the battlefield. Now, he can make only a belated confession: "All along I knew I should have been saying, "I agree with my wife, absolutely." On his eightieth birthday, the old man finally summons up the courage to denounce his father's memory and the warrior Germany of his youth, shouting "Down with the honor of our fathers and our grandfathers and our great-grandfathers!"

The destroyer of the Abbey is Heinrich's own son, Robert, the representative of that generation of Germans who grew up during the Nazi period and faced combat duty in the war under the epigraph "Adam, wo warst du?" At first glance, Robert's willingness to blow up the Abbey to clear the field of fire between the German and American armies, even though the war was almost over, would seem to express the destruction of the past by the godless present. This, however, is not the meaning of Böll's complex religious vision here, as we shall see.

Robert's recollective monologues take him back to a key date in his formative years, the day of "Faehmel's Home Run, July 14, 1935," when he saw one player viciously hitting another with a ball. Robert takes his stand by befriending the victimized Schrella and his companions, who call themselves "Lambs," who have sworn never to take the "Host of the Beast" to their lips. The Lambs and the Beasts: we are back to that essential split between the crucified and the hangmen which marked Böll's earlier works; more specifically, the Lambs and the Beasts can be said to refer to the anti-Nazis and the Nazis. Not only does Robert take the oath against the Beast; he is also beaten up by the fascistic bully Nettlinger and his crowd. He meets another "Lamb," Schrella's sister Edith, makes love to her, and later marries her, to the embarrassment of his family. Political persecution forces Robert to take refuge abroad until his return is negotiated on the condition of his taking no part in political activity and his agreeing to immediate induction after completion of examinations. During his brief apprenticeship with the Lambs, Robert had seen others victimized. While at war he constantly remembers those 'crucified' by firing squads or falling bombs: the young anarchist Ferdi Progulske, the waiter Groll, the boy who had slipped messages into the letter box, his wife Edith. It is for them that he blows up the Abbey: the world must accept the truth of evil, not console itself in visions of the past: "He had got himself trained as a demolitions expert, later trained demolition squads himself, implanting formulas which contained exactly what he wanted: dust and rubble and revenge . . . A monument for the lambs no one had fed." Implicitly, Böll is asking whether good can come out of destruction, whether this deeply motivated gesture is really as noble as Robert pretends.

The German temperament has often been characterized as being in perpetual tension between a profoundly destructive energy and an almost compulsive need for order. Robert's post-war existence is a frightening attempt to replace destruction with order (and indeed, his father's thousands of breakfasts with paprika cheese at the Café Kroner reveal a similar need). Every morning at half-past nine he plays billiards in the Prince Heinrich Hotel, and the game, reminiscent of his work in demolitions computations, allows him to sublimate his emotions into mathematical equations: "And the swirl of lines was all angularly bound by geometric law and physics. Energy of the blow imparted to the ball by cue, plus a little friction, question of degree, the brain taking note of it, and behold, impulse was converted into momentary figures." The psychological tension underlying this attempt at sublimation is clearly unbearable. With the relaxing assistance of numerous cognacs, Robert confesses his past (especially the secret of the destruction of the Abbey) to the page boy Hugo, his special guardian angel.

Böll has mixed feelings about priests, as we have seen. Hugo, the darling of the female clients of the hotel ("Your face is worth a fortune, pure gold . . . Why won't you be the Lamb of God in my new religion?") becomes the unwitting vehicle of religious revelation for Robert Faehmel. Hugo is the child-like confessor who has retained his purity and can therefore offer absolution. In its complex ritual, the game of billiards is almost liturgical. the many glasses of cognac seem strangely sacramental. But the confessor himself confesses, and the story he tells of his drunken mother, his truancy, and of the constant beatings he received from masters and schoolmates alike (compare the childhood of Bernanos' Curé d'Ambricourt in *Diary of a Country Priest*) defines Hugo's symbolic function in *Billiards* . . .

> "And while they were working me over I used to think, why did Christ die, anyway? What good did it ever do me? . . . You know what they used to holler at me when they were beating me up? *God's little lamb.* That was my nickname . . . . There's been a war a little while before, and they asked me if I'd ever been in a cemetery where it said 'Fallen' on the gravestones, the way we Germans say it when we mean 'Killed in battle.' I told them, yes, I'd seen 'Fallen.' Then what did I think 'Fallen' meant? I said I imagined that the people buried there had died from falling down."

Fallen has yet another meaning, of course, but Hugo is not only naive, he is also pure. At the end of the novel, Robert decides to adopt the fatherless Hugo as his elective son (his own son Joseph, who is engaged in the reconstruction of the Abbey, is seen speeding along the Autobahn with his girlfriend at his side). Novelistically, the adoption seems unsatisfying; one can only assume it has been placed in the narrative to provide a symbol of Robert's reconciliation with his past guilt, his acceptance of Christ as a Redeemer, and his realization that innocence is possible.

Germany cannot forget its past that easily, however; the spiritual struggle between the crucified and the hangmen continues, will continue. Two key figures from Robert's past are brought together in a memorable scene: Schrella, whose persecution during the game of rounders had brought Faehmel to the "Lambs," and Nettlinger, the leader of those who had partaken of the "Sacrament of the Beast." Schrella was exiled for most of the Hitler years and has only now returned to Germany with his name still on the wanted list. He is immediately arrested for suspicious behavior, though Nettlinger's intercession effects his prompt release from prison (Böll softens Nettlinger's brutal role in the novel by making him the author of quite a few charitable actions—he is not a bloodthirsty fanatic but a "decent Nazi," and therefore all the more despicable). Schrella views the new Germany as a girl grown rather fat, with glands working overtime, and married to a rich, hard-working man who has a car and a country house. Nettlinger is the image of that new prosperity: fine Havana cigars, a chauffeur, a taste for good food. In the dining room of the Prince Heinrich Hotel (where his father had been a waiter), Schrella gets his revenge by eating with his hands, reaching across the table and asking to have the leftovers of his chicken dinner wrapped. Symbolically, he is avenged when he, not Nettlinger, wins access to Robert.

The real seer in *Billiards at Half-Past Nine* is Johanna Kilb Faehmel, the wife of Heinrich and mother of Robert, though her role as a prophetess of truth is at times blurred by the profusion of internal monologues. It is typical of Böll (and of much recent German literature, as Theodore Ziolkowski has shown in *Neophilologus*) that Johanna's insights are those of a "madwoman" (Böll's "Clown" is a reincarnation of the same type). Her behavior, both political and religious, has always been so exemplary that she is considered insane by her compatriots. In 1917, she spoke out against "that fool of a Kaiser" and tore up a pompous patriotic poem— "Hindenburg! On to the fight!"—which her son had memorized. She gave away her allotments of food from the Abbey farms during both world wars. When, in 1941, she went to the freight cars to try to go along with the Jews, the time had come to commit her: by then, she was "the kind of woman you only see in the old pictures in the museums." To celebrate her husband's eightieth birthday she leaves the asylum, but she cannot be reconciled to the world; when from the hotel room window she witnesses a parade of the "Fighting Veterans League" headed by an official on a white horse, the whole of Germany's warrior past becomes a renewed present in her deranged but clairvoyant mind. She shoots the man on horseback, wounding him slightly. Her shot, like Böll's novel, is a protest against the dechristianized world of the Nettlingers and veterans. Throughout the book, we are assaulted by the recurring leitmotif of violence, the bleeding boar hanging in Gretz's butcher shop; Johanna, with Edith, Schrella, Jochen; and Hugo is the *Lamb of God qui tollis peccata mundi.*

Hans Schnier, the narrator-hero of *The Clown,* Böll's finest creation, I believe, is another eccentric seeker of truth, and unmasker of hypocrisy, and in his strange, half-mad way, a modern saint. Böll has worked on translations of Salinger's *The Catcher in the Rye* and *Franny & Zooey;* and Holden Caulfield and the clown are spiritual brothers. For Schnier, sincere irreverence is a form of sanctity; the orthodox are uniformly "Christian worms," as he calls the head of the Christian Education Society. His reversal of values is clearly shown in his credo: "I believe that the living are dead, and that the dead live, not the way Protestants and Catholics believe it." The same might have been the credo of the mad Johanna Faehmel. Schnier describes himself as a clown with no church affiliation. His parents, devout Protestants, subscribed to the postwar fashion of denominational tolerance and sent him to a Catholic school. Hans still remembers the hymns, and for a long time he used to sing the *Tantum Ergo* or the *Litany of Loreto* in the bathtub to overcome depressions and headaches. Now alcohol has replaced the hymn: "A clown who takes to drink falls faster than a drunk tile-layer topples off the roof."

As author, Böll is here himself "the clown," the unmasker, the satirizer of the newly progressive Catholic Church whose members seem "to be crocheting themselves loincloths out of Thomas Aquinas, St. Francis of Assisi, Bonaventure and Pope Leo XIII, loincloths which of course failed to cover their nakedness, for . . . there was no one there who wasn't earning at least fifteen hundred marks a month." Language itself is subject to radical distrust, for Hans' art is based on communication through silence, gesture and facial expression. Other people's ideas or opinions are expressed in Hans' consciousness with quotation marks around them, striking a constantly false note in the receiver's mind ("Jewish spirituality, metaphysical horror, Catholic air, the initiated, committed," etc.), alien notions with a false sense of self-importance clichés lacking integrity. Hans feels that "we had been talking at cross-purposes for five years." His conversation with Mrs. Kalick, a woman with "that kind of attractiveness that makes you wonder whether she is alive or merely wound up" is likened to "feeding coins into a machine. Mrs. Schnier tries to make language less real by removing all the harsher, unrefined guttural sounds from her sentences. There are, in fact, only four Catholics left in the world, we are repeatedly told: Pope John, Alec Guinness, Marie (the clown's mistress), and Gregory, an old Negro boxer now earning a meager living as a strong man in vaudeville. When Marie yields at last to the blandishments of Prelate Sommerwild and his fashionable Catholics, she is castigated by her foresaken lover as a new first lady of German Catholicism, another Jacqueline Kennedy! Even the clown's own brother, Leo, is unable to help, for the monks whom Leo has joined are apparently always in the refectory eating cabbage or desserts. "If our era deserves a name, it would have to be called the era of prostitution," the clown concludes.

As was the case with Robert Faehmel, victimization of the innocent is for Schnier a formative experience. His sister Henrietta happily volunteered for anti-aircraft duty as though it were a school outing; she never came back. And Hans wonders what his business-like father would look like if seen through a live Henrietta's eyes:

I could only see her as being desperate, doing something realists would find outrageous because they have no imagination. Pouring a cocktail down the collar of one of the innumerable presidents, or ploughing her car into the Mercedes of one of the head hypocrites. What else could she have done if she hadn't been able to print or make ashtrays on a potter's wheel? She would be bound to feel it, as I felt it, wherever there was life, this invisible wall where money ceased to be there to be spent, where it became inviolate and dwelled in tabernacles in the form of figures and columns.

Henrietta, however, had died, her mother explains, "defending Our Sacred German Soil from the Jewish Yankees." The originator of that phrase, the Hitler Youth leader, Herbert Kalick, was thereupon denounced as a "Nazi swine" by the eleven-year-old Hans, who was sentenced to dig a tank trap as punishment. From that day on, Hans' parents ceased to exist for him. His entire adult existence as a clown is an attempt to retain his childlike courage, to answer the inner call to unmask the world of prosperous businessmen and hypocritical pious ladies embodied by his parents: his father, a wealthy coal merchant whose profits never diminished, and his mother, now a leading member of the "Fellowship for the Reconciliation of Racial Differences" which makes an annual pilgrimage to Anne Frank's House. Throughout the novel, the image of the sixteen-year-old Henrietta reappears whenever Hans meets the newly crucified victims of West Germany's postwar prosperity.

The central experience in Hans Schnier's twenty-seven-year itinerary of disillusionment is his "marriage" to Marie Derkum. I use the sacramental term advisedly, because Hans' reversal of values is such that he constantly refers to himself as monogamous and deplores her "adultery" and "fornication" with her husband Züpfner: Prelate Sommerwild is "acting the pimp." Since Hans had become so estranged from his own parents that he thought of them as running a foster home, he had put himself under the protection of Mr. Derkum, an ex-Catholic, a poor, honest man, and worked in his shop. There he had met and seduced Marie. The consummation of their love, as Hans remembers it, was a moment of purest innocence. But Marie has been raised a Catholic, and after traveling around with the clown for a few years her association with conventional believers

leads her to yearn for a sanctified marriage. Despite numerous miscarriages, Marie worries about questions of doctrine: will her children
be trained as Catholics? is she living in sin? Schnier refuses to give in
to what he calls "Catholic blackmail" and denounces the influence of
the Catholic Study Group on his concubine: "Everything was fine
with Marie as long as she was worrying about my own soul, but you
people taught her to worry about her own soul." Marie runs away
to marry the conventional believer, Züpfner, to breathe some *Catholic air.* The clown is left alone with his bottle of brandy and his
memories, like Beckett's Krapp. If he had failed in his career and in
his "marriage," his very failure constitutes his purity and makes of
him a prophet of truth, an "early Christian" amid the pagans of the
New Germany.

What is a clown? A clown is the messenger of the visionary
games and insights of children, the purest form of theatre. Hans himself only likes children's movies, is as frank and uninhibited as a
child, and is always playing his part ("A child, too, never takes time
off as a child."). To be a clown is to respond to a *vocatus*, and it is
small wonder that Hans' affection for Pope John is explained with
touching irreverence: "There was something of a wise old clown
about him too, and after all the figure of Harlequin had originated
in Bergamo." Above all, the clown, in his act, mirrors the fall of man.
Schnier's routines range from his impressions of a bankers' meeting
to his own preferred "absurdities of everyday life." During his years
of relative success, the clown's function as mirror remained too
benevolent; his career depended precisely on those whom he was
ridiculing—the wealthy Catholic Pharisees and the complacent
businessmen. Despite his poetic gift of detecting odors (usually of
corruption) over the telephone, Schnier did not become a real clown
until Marie left him. Now, as he explains: "I am a clown and I collect moments." Most of the novel consists of reminiscences of past
persecution and of sarcastic telephone appeals for help to those
Catholics Schnier most despises. As in most of Böll's works, there is
in *The Clown* a regular pattern of alternating nostalgia and savage
caricature, as Schnier struggles toward attainment of his own self-
definition: "Neither a Catholic, nor a Protestant, but a Clown."
As all his supposed friends desert him, or at best try to force him to
take up his conventional career as public entertainer again, Schnier

turns inward toward a most peculiar form of prayer, perhaps a form of madness not unlike Johanna Faehmel's.

Carefully putting on a heavy layer of makeup until the grease cracks, "showing features like the face of an excavated statue," he steps back from the mirror and "looks more deeply (into himself) and at the same time further away." He picks up his guitar (Marie and his agent had thought the guitar undignified) and walks toward the central station. It is Carnival time and on the station steps a group of "matadors" and "Spanish donnas" are waiting for a taxi. The clown puts his hat down beside him and begins to sing:

> Catholic politics in Bonn
> Are no concern of poor Pope John
> Let them holler, let them go,
> Eeeny, meeny, miny mo.

A stranger drops a coin into the hat, and the clown goes on singing. His song is in a strange way a prayer in praise of simplicity. Hans Schnier has become a prophetic singer like the Negro street balladeer in *Acquainted with the Night*. Somehow at Carnival time ("there is no better hiding place for a professional than among amateurs") people are more genuine than in their real, but totally hollow, day-to-day lives. A faceless, disguised stranger has responded to the song with the ancient Christian gesture of spontaneous charity. For a brief moment, the hypocrisy of a world where one must pray to console God yields to the vision of possible harmony contained in the cacophonic hymn of a nonbeliever. Once again, Böll's epigraph to a novel (this time from *Romans* XV: 21) conveys the essence of his own song: "To whom he was not spoken of, they shall see: and they that have not heard shall understand."

Chapter VI

Children's Faces: Graham Greene

If a perceptive, though irreverent, critic once called Graham Greene's novels "great bad books," one of my own students put the matter more crudely in dismissing *Brighton Rock* because "it's like reading a *Hardy Boys* book." The stock situations and facile black-and-white characterizations of juvenile fiction, from *Tom Brown's Schooldays* through Dixon's glorification of "hardy" boys, are indeed a basic ingredient in Greene's formula for serious adult novels: "[Mr. Colleoni] was a small Jew with a neat round belly ... and his eyes gleamed like raisins." Clearly a villain! And when that suspiciously foreign name is compared to such sterling first names as Rose and Pinkie, Greene does indeed seem to have stacked the allegorical odds. And yet even in his first "Catholic novel," *Brighton Rock*, of 1938, the novelist moves away from primary colors and into blends and half-tints (He was fond of saying that the world was not black-and-white, but black-and-grey): *Rose, Pinkie Brown, Molly Pink*. For Greene, the adolescent, the apprentice criminal, the school boy are in a transitional world between the purity of the babe and the malevolence of the adult. When Pinkie returns to his birthplace at "Paradise Piece," he meets a crippled child:

> . . . it was like the dreadful appeal of innocence, but there was not innocence: you had to go back a long way further before you got innocence; innocence was a slobbering mouth, a toothless gum pulling at the teats, perhaps not even that; innocence was the ugly cry of birth.

Those of us who have interpreted Greene's work in the light of the Christological children in Dostoevsky and Bernanos have perhaps unwittingly attenuated his very literal belief in original sin, a belief that owes much to his interest in psychoanalysis with its emphasis on infantile sexuality. We have forgotten the children in Brighton's amusement tunnel with their paper sailor hats marked "I'm no angel." The adolescent, acting out the ancient schoolboy pattern of initiation into the class, of making the team, is suspended between innocence and guilt, between heaven and hell:

> The gulls which had stood like candles down the beach rose and cried under the promenade. The old man found a boot and stowed it in his sack and a gull dropped from the parade and swept through the iron nave of the Palace Pier, white and purposeful in the obscurity: *half vulture and half dove*. In the end one always had to learn (italics mine).

And in the lounge-bar of "Lureland":

> Siphons stood about on blue-topped tables, and on the stained-glass windows medieval ships tossed on cold curling waves. Somebody had broken the hands off one of the statuettes—or perhaps it was made like that, something classical in white drapery, *a symbol of victory or despair*. (italics mine) The Boy rang a bell and a boy of his own age came out of the public bar to take his order: they were oddly alike and allusively different—narrow shoulders, thin face, they bristled like dogs at the sight of each other.

Those who are only in the ante-room of damnation, for whom all hope has not yet been abandoned, are invariably seen as adolescent schoolboys. The decrepit, yellow-toothed lawyer, Mr. Drewitt, knows that Brighton is hell; he uses the same words, spoken by Marlowe's Mephistopheles, that Greene himself will apply to the "Metroland loneliness" surrounding his school in the *Prologue* to *The Lawless Roads* (1939): "Why, this is Hell, nor are we out of it." Drewitt's shameful urge to expose himself ("No money can heal a mind diseased. This is Hell . . . How much could you spare?") would seem to damn him irrevocably, were it not for the vestiges of adolescence which the author carefully leaves him. Drewitt is "an old Lancaster boy" with a photo of the school group on the wall and memories of field days with Harrow. Like a schoolboy, Drewitt has "grubby and bitten nails" on the shaky hands "which were the instruments of pleasure." His addiction to masturbation strangely becomes that of puberty rather than the vice of the married adult who watches the typists going by and then dreams of "embracing their little portable machines." In this most Freudian of Greene's novels (he once called the time of his own analysis "perhaps the happiest months of my life), the proselyte author forgives his characters more than they, Jansenists to the core, are willing to forgive themselves.

"I write for the child I used to be," Bernanos was fond of saying. Graham Greene, for whom Christ's *revelasti ea parvulis* prefigures Freudian theory, writes for the lonely and tormented schoolboy he had once been. "I was, I suppose, thirteen years old," he writes in the improbable beginning of his 1939 Mexican journal, *The Lawless Roads:*

> And so faith came to one—shapelessly, without dogma, a presence above a croquet lawn, something associated with violence, cruelty, evil across the way. One began to believe in Heaven because one believed in Hell, but for a long while it was only hell one could picture with a certain intimacy—the pitchpine partitions of dormitories where everybody was never quiet at the same time; lavatories without locks . . . walks in pairs up the suburban roads; no solitude anywhere, at any time.

The initiation into belief, into acceptance of the reality of Hell, comes through the apprenticeship in the world of adults that we call adolescence but which for Greene seems to go back to the traumas of childhood. The boy Philip, in the revealing story, *The Basement Room* (1936), loves to keep secrets and to listen to Baines telling stories, but discovers that the sharer becomes an accomplice in a sordid adult plot and that the childhood adventure stories turn into novels of adultery:

> A kind of embittered happiness and self-pity made him cry; he was lost; there wouldn't be any more secrets to keep. he surrendered responsibility once and for all. Let grown-up people keep to their world and he would keep to his, safe in the small garden between the plane-trees. "In the lost childhood of Judas Christ was betrayed";

> you could almost see *the small unformed face* hardening into the
> deep dilettante *selfishness of age.* (italics mine).

"The lost childhood of Judas." That line from AE's *Germinal,*
which became the title of one of Greene's most moving essays, seems
to combine psychoanalysis with theology. Can one explain, and
perchance excuse, the archetypal betrayal by the determinism of
a trauma repressed or buried in a longlost childhood? Or does the
very loss of childhood constitute a formation of a Judas? Both are
doubtless true, yet we should never forget that even childhood is
theologically far removed from the "ugly cry of birth" that is innocence. As Ida Arnold says to Rose who had naively maintained that
"People change" (Greene has cleverly reversed the roles here, making
the non-believing Ida the spokesman for the Catholic truth of
original sin):

> "Oh, no, they don't. Look at me. I've never changed. It's like those
> sticks of rock: bite it all the way down, you'd still read Brighton.
> That's human nature." She breathed mournfully over Rose's face—
> a sweet and winy breath.
> "Confession . . .repentance," Rose whispered.
> "That's just religion," the woman said. "Believe me, it's the world
> we got to deal with."

And so the Philip of *The Basement Room* will not be able to keep
to his safe world in the small garden; even with the dilettante selfish-
ness of age he will keep his small unformed face, but his essential
sinfulness (to be born is to take the first step toward sin, toward
adulthood and death) is as present in every fiber of his being as the
name of Brighton in that Churchless "rock."

II

> The possibility of damnation is so immense a relief in a world
> of electoral reform, plebiscites, sex reform and dress reform, that
> damnation itself is an immediate form of salvation—of salvation
> from the ennui of modern life, because it at least gives some
> significance to living.

T. S. Eliot's oft-quoted remarks define the two forms of purgatory in Greene's imperfect, and for that reason all the more revealing, first Catholic novel. There is the purgatory of the adolescent who by definition *is* "Possibility of damnation" and therefore possibility of salvation; there is the purgatory of the lukewarm, of the non-believer or unbaptized, who will be spewn forth, as the Apocalypse foretells, or cast into the circle of a Hell which leads nowhere. And these two forms are physically rendered: there are the still growing children or adolescents, and there are the fully grown adults. "A mystic in a primitive or wild state," Claudel once called that prototypical adolescent, Arthur Rimbaud. Mr. Colleoni is not only the evil Jew of Victorian edifying literature for juveniles, he is also the successful adult (Colleoni, the Venetian warrior, does sound rather like *coglione* too—the very emblem of impending manhood). He owns the world Pinkie seeks to penetrate, "the whole visible world, that is: cash registers and policemen and prostitutes, Parliament and the laws which say 'this is Right and this is Wrong.' " Every trait both in his setting and in his person confirms an impression of fullness and maturity. The Cosmopolitan Hotel (where else would an Italo-Jewish ganglord be found?) has an acre of deep carpet, deep velvet couches, overweight clients in furs and jewels; Colleoni himself has a round belly, plump thighs, a gold lighter and long cigar. Small wonder that Greene constantly refers to Pinkie allegorically as "the Boy" ("You are not Mr. P. Brown?" Colleoni had asked. "I expected someone a good deal older."); for the relationship between the "two criminals" quickly becomes that of father to rebellious son, of schoolmaster to insolent pupil. "You're wasting your time, my child," Mr. Colleoni says after the Boy had threatened violence. The same parental attitude, superficially affectionate but profoundly corrupting, marks Ida's encounters with Rose as she tries to get the evidence to convict Pinkie of murdering Hale: "Pardon, dear. You see we can get along all right when we are together. I've never had a child of my own and somehow I've taken to you. You're a sweet thing." Late in the novel, Ida practices an even crueler deception, literally passing herself off as Rose's mother to gain admittance to her rooms:

> "I know." Rose ran upstairs; it was the biggest triumph you could ever expect: to greet your mother for the first time in your own house; ask her to sit down on your own chair, to look at each other

with an equal experience. There was nothing now, Rose felt, her
mother knew about men she didn't know: that was the reward for
the painful ritual upon the bed. She flung the door gladly open and
there was the woman.

Ida even moves across the floor as if she intended to take Rose in
her arms, explaining "Why, you poor little thing, I pity you." Pity
is that adult substitute for Christlike compassion which will distort
Scobie's self-imposed Calvary in *The Heart of the Matter,* as we shall
see. In contrast, Pinkie looks at the greying hair of Spicer, his next
victim with "no pity at all; he wasn't old enough for pity."

If we examine Greene's careful presentation of Ida's total
physicality, the same impression of maternal fullness and maturity
is reinforced. (What Ida Arnold represents in the theological structure
of the novel has, of course, been the subject of much critical scru-
tiny, and will concern me only obliquely.) Ida smells of soap and
wine, comfort and peace and a slow physical enjoyment, with her
"big breasts, which had never suckled a child of her own," "her large
cool pastry-making hands," her "big, tipsy mouth." Ida, as her name
indicates, is the embodiment of the plenitude of life. She accepts the
comfort of the deep couch and the gaudy furnishings of her place of
assignation with Mr. Corkery "like an aphrodisiac in her tea." Above
all, Ida Arnold joyfully accepts sex: "It doesn't do anyone any harm
that I know of. It's human nature." As she undresses in surroundings
so similar to Colleoni's ("big padded pleasure dome of a bedroom,
deep soft rug, red velvet hangings"), she thinks of popular phrases
"A Night of Love," "You Only Live Once," and works "her plump
toes" in the rug. At the very moment that Pinkie is *buying* Rose
from her moody parents (they ask for guineas not pounds in one of
the true revelations of grown-up venality) and dreading the inevita-
bility of consummation ("the horrifying act of a desire he didn't
feel"), Ida is consuming the Host of *her* religion of uninhibited eroti-
cism, a phallic god indeed:

> [She] bit an eclair and the cream spurted between the large front
> teeth. She laughed a little thickly in the Pompadour Boudoir and
> said: "I haven't had as much money to spend since I left Tom."
> She took another bite and a wedge of cream settled on the plump
> tongue.

In contrast to Ida's "Bacchic and bawdy" cult and ample physical endowment, Pinkie and Rose are slight, almost monastic (he had wanted to be a priest: "They know what's what. They keep away."), and physically and psychically incomplete. Pinkie has little experience of the adult world despite his career in the protective rackets:

> He knew everything in theory, nothing in practice; he was only old with the knowledge of other people's lusts, those of strangers who wrote their desires on the walls in public lavatories. He knew the moves, he'd never played the game.

Brighton Rock narrates Pinkie's conversion from theory to practice. "I don't drink," he admitted in the first pages; he will begin drinking and shortly before his death downs two double brandies. "I don't bet," he tells Spicer, but he will gamble on his salvation by committing suicide. He acquires the habit of lying (Greene explains that "he wasn't used to lying"). He is taunted by Spicer's girl, Sylvie: "I bet you don't go with girls either," yet much of the novel is devoted to his initiation into sex: from a kiss ("his mouth missed hers and recoiled. He's never yet kissed a girl") to the marriage-bed (" 'It's Saturday night,' he said with a bitter taste on his tongue, 'It's time for bed.' "). Each movement toward adulthood is accompanied by the imagery of juvenile fiction. When Pinkie reviews his brief but effective career in murder, Greene tells us "He had *graduated* in pain . . . . He had a sense now that the murders of Hale and Spicer were trivial acts, a *boys' game,* and he had put away *childish things*" (italics mine). A Wedding night in mortal sin fills him with "a kind of gloomy hilarity and pride. He saw himself now as a full-grown man for whom the angels wept." His last gesture of satanic defiance, the recording of his message of hatred and damnation to Rose, forces him to absent himself from his gangland mission, giving him "the sense of playing truant from his proper work—he should be at school but he hadn't learned his lesson." And in a simile that reveals the author's essentially adult pity toward the Boy, Pinkie is described after his wedding as being "like a child with haemophilia: every contact drew blood" (*He* is the Virgin whose deflowering leads to a blood disease).

If one tries to reconstitute a portrait of Pinkie from the details scattered throughout the novel by Greene, the obsession with adolescence betrayed by the opening of *The Lawless Roads* becomes all the more striking. The nervousness of puberty shows in his bitten nails (Pinkie's first victim, Hale, who had been both figurative son and figurative lover to Ida, had bitten nails and inky fingers), in his reflexive gesture of "licking an indelible pencil, his mouth was stained purple at the corners," in his slight tic "through the soft chicken down, where you might have expected a dimple." His face is "like a child's badgered, confused, betrayed," and the years of hard experience are called "fake years." In those rare moments of self-revelation when Pinkie sings, it is "in his spoilt boy's voice" or in "his high adolescent voice." His repressed sexuality finds an outlet in cruelty, as he systematically tears an insect's wings off (" 'She loves me,' he said, 'she loves me not.' ") or crushes a wounded moth underfoot; or else in uncontrolled fits of rage as he shouts "I want service," smashing a salt sprinkler down on the table with "a little spurt of vicious anger." Only one form of experience seems to take him beyond the immediate physical impulse and that is music. For Ida Arnold, music (" 'One night in an alley,' [she] sings, 'Lord Rothschild said to me' ") had been an incitement to the physical; for Pinkie music is a dangerous enemy, stirring in his brain "like poetry," speaking to him of "things he didn't understand." Small wonder that he is unwillingly prompted to sing softly the words of the Mass (of the *Agnus dei qui tollis peccata mundi, dona nobis pacem,* particularly) by even the most vulgar popular songs: "Music was the nearest he knew to sorrow." Pinkie weeps in a movie when he hears a leading man moaning "I know in my heart you're divine", the trite words suddenly assuming a literal meaning to the apostate Catholic, like "a vision of release to an imprisoned man." Christ was in the music as much as in the Host; here was an area of adult experience that was not pity but compassion, was far removed from the physicality of Colleoni and of Ida:

> Only the music made him uneasy, the cat-gut vibrating in the heart; it was like nerves losing their freshness, it was like age coming on, other people's experience battering on the brain.

What irony then that the record he cuts should not be the song of "something loving" requested by Rose, but the message of hatred, "the worst horror of all."

The record will be Rose's future, and that betrayal was prepared, like Christ's own, in Pinkie's lost childhood. Two literally formative traumatic experiences constitute Pinkie's psychic inheritance and provide the matrices for the novel's imagery. When Pinkie drives with Rose along the road to Peacehaven (again the Catholic novelist's penchant for allegorical onomastics!), stopping at Lureland to prepare the bogus suicide pact which will eliminate her as potential witness against him, he encounters Piker, his double and a former schoolmate from Catholic-school days. Pinkie's tortured past as victim and would-be priest comes back to him when he sips a double brandy in a bizarre communion parody:

> The Boy rang a bell and a boy of his own age came out of the public bar to take his order; they were oddly alike and allusively different—narrow shoulders, thin face, they bristled like dogs at the sight of each other.
>
> . . . .
>
> He looked with loathing into the past—a cracked bell ringing, a child weeping under the cane.
>
> . . . .
>
> . . . fake years slipped away—he was whisked back towards the unhappy playground.

One has the feeling that Pinkie's career in murder is a reenactment of the playground scene where he stabbed a 'bullied brat' with the dividers as well as a revenge for beatings received from parental figures in the school—characteristically, he acts upon ineffectual, childlike figures: Hale, Spicer, Rose. "He had graduated in pain: first the school dividers had been left behind, then the razor . . . Murder had only led to this—this corruption." The corruption is sex, "the frightening weekly exercise of his parents, bouncing and ploughing." If you were ignorant of "that one dirty scramble," he thinks, you knew nothing.

Pinkie will come to knowledge, if not to pleasure, but the pervasive sense of a prolonged puberty is conveyed by a carefully contrived series of phallic substitutes, actually masturbatory in quality, which distort Pinkie's erotic energies. His assaults by stabbing and slashing, his stabbing of Rose's arm with his one unbitten nail, his constant fingering and "tickling" of the vitriol bottle which he keeps in his pocket, are distinctly sexual gestures. When he fails so miserably in his first sexual "scramble" with Sylvie in the back seat of a car ("he was aware of nausea and retched. Marry he thought, hell, no; I'd rather hang"), Greene draws attention to the Boy's pointed shoes slipping on the wet tiles near a swimming pool where two lovers were swimming together. These shoes, mentioned repeatedly, cannot help but remind us again of the author's more than passing infatuation with psychoanalysis. So too do, here in a comically vulgar way, the gang's wedding presents to Pinkie and Rose: a tiny doll's commode in the shape of a radio set labelled "the smallest A.-1 two-valve receiving set in the world," and a mustard pot shaped like a lavatory seat with the legend "For me and my girl." These images of displacement lead inevitably to the real thing, to direct experience. "You're growing up, Pinkie, like your father," Dallow says after the wedding:

> "Like my father . . . " The Boy was shaken again with his nocturnal Saturday disgust. He couldn't blame his father now . . . it was what you came to . . . you got mixed up, and then, he supposed the habit grew . . . you gave yourself away weekly.

Pinkie's entire career in violent crime had been an attempt to ward off, to defer sexual experience. Kite the gangleader had picked him up, adopted him. But Kite had died. Pinkie had prolonged Kite's existence, "not touching liquor, biting his nails in the Kite way, until *she* came and altered everything." For Pinkie, Kite was the father unblemished by the horror of Saturday night procreation (Freud has written often and well of that shattering discovery by the child that "father and mother" are "lovers" to each other). The death of the father-substitute left him with the legacy of "his duty never to leave for strange acres" and a mission of revenge. Ironically, it will be the "maternal" Ida (" 'What, she? She's old enough to be my mother.' "), who will drive the Boy to self-destruction at the very moment Rose may already be carrying his child.

The movement of the novel from adolescence to the malevolence of adulthood is symbolically reversed by Pinkie's death. As he mutilates his own face with vitriol and leaps over the cliff, "he looked half his size, doubled up in appalling agony; it was as if the flames had literally got him and he shrank—shrank into a schoolboy flying in panic and pain, scrambling over a fence, running on." Rose whose innocence had been detailed repeatedly ("She didn't even know the name of a drink"), becomes a mystical reincarnation of the childlike Virgin thanks to her husband's self-immolation. She too had lived an apprenticeship ("She was like a child in a new school . . . "), but her grossly enlarged and distorted image reflected in a bottle of Extra-Stout ("It seemed to carry an enormous weight of responsibility") is transformed into that of one of the dolls ("like Virgins in a church repository") that Pinkie had won in the shooting gallery. In the confessional an old priest begs her: "Pray for me, my child."

III

The excessively contrived network of children's faces in *Brighton Rock* reflect the author's pity for his creation. I get the feeling that Greene is trying too hard, that with blatant allegory in onomastics, an addiction to Manicheanism in the reversal of the ethics of the schoolboy novel (here the self-designated "good" are ultimately "evil" and cast into hell, whereas those who commit murder and suicide achieve at least an initial groping toward salvation), he is still too close to his own experience of faith coming through belief in Hell, thereby remaining too eager to communicate that strategy of salvation to a reader who probably shares the modern worldly ethic of an Ida Arnold. In his mature fiction, Greene retreats somewhat from the temptation of the Manichees (or of De Maistre): the saint is linked to the sinner, not to the criminal.

In what I see as his finest creation, *The Heart of the Matter*, the novelist has shifted the burden of bearing adult pity for the childlike onto his protagonist, Scobie. It will be Scobie's penchant (instead of Greene's as author) to see "childrens' faces" everywhere.

In a crucial scene, Scobie actually becomes the "narrator" of a *mysterium iniquitatis* worthy of the schoolboy-novel liturgy of *Brighton Rock*. A Protestant missionary asks him to read a story to a little boy rescued from a torpedoed boat, assuring him that the novels in her library are not "novels," but safe. The titles include *Twenty Years in the Mission Field, Lost and Found, The Narrow Way,* happy-ending books, in short. (Like our other Catholic novelists Greene loves to satirize the Pharisees and *bien-pensants.*) Scobie selects *A Bishop among the Bantus,* and in telling it makes it into a boyhood tale of Arthur Bishop, a secret agent of the British Government, who lets himself be captured by the Bantus in order to discover their secret passwords, hiding places and plans of raids. He falls in love with the daughter of the captain of the Bantus and turns "soppy." But there are a lot of fights and murder before the end, Scobie insists. This is, of course, a foreshadowing of Scobie's own betrayal by Wilson. Wilson, "the old boy" who subscribed to the *Old Downhamian,* the alumni magazine, will be tracking down the "adult" Scobie.

The novel opens with Wilson's arrival in the colony, as he sits "stroking his very young moustache" and looking down at the world of vultures and pye-dogs, of brothels and corruption that Scobie has long been familiar with in his job as deputy police commissioner. Wilson, seen by Scobie the adult, is very much like Pinkie viewed by Greene in *Brighton Rock:*

> There was something defenseless, it seemed to Scobie, in his whole attitude: he stood there waiting for people to be friendly or unfriendly—he didn't seem to expect one reaction more than another. He was like a dog. Nobody had yet drawn on his face the lines that make a human being.

But then Scobie finds the childlike and pitiable in everyone, as we shall see. The author himself is rather harder on Wilson, while remaining faithful to his basic pattern of imagery. The police spy has "bald pink knees," a smooth face "pink and healthy, plump and hopeless," wears his mustache "like a club tie." Wilson's friendship with his fellow Downhamian, the middle-aged Harris, is a desperate attempt to organize chaotic experience by schoolboy rules. A cockroach hunt with a slipper and a scorecard ("The Cockroach Championship") becomes an obstacle to their relationship when Wilson refuses to abide by the rules set up by "the inventor of the game":

> "My rules are the Queensberry rules in this town."
> "They won't be for long," Wilson threatened.

Despite their squabbling, Harris and Wilson decide to "room together with thoughts of an Old Downhamian dinner rejected by the irritable and defensive Wilson:

> He was one of those, it seemed to Harris, who always knew what was on: who gave advance information on extra haves; who knew why old So-and-So had not turned up to school, and what the row brewing at the Masters' special meeting was about. A few weeks ago he had been a new boy whom Harris had been delighted to befriend, to show around . . . But Harris from his first year at school had been fated to see how quickly new boys grew up.

In fact Wilson is really more like the transfer student who had been sent down elsewhere. While Harris (who had meanwhile composed a newsy letter for the *Old Downhamian*) sips barley water with lime, Wilson drinks whisky. He goes to the brothel "impelled by a passion of curiosity more than of lust" and after a momentary revulsion he surrenders: "he felt as though his dead veins would bleed again." The so-called "new boy" had clearly served his apprenticeship in adult evil elsewhere. Unlike Pinkie who learns deviousness in the course of the novel, Wilson's profession was to lie. He lies particularly about his love of poetry ("he absorbed it secretly—like a drug"), which becomes the basis for his love for Scobie's wife, Louise. The "schoolboy" falls in love with the "headmaster's" wife, one might say ("Have I really found a friend?" he wonders). Wilson publishes his declaration of love, the poem *Tristram* (!) in the school magazine, and other signs of schoolboy infatuation abound: when Louise slaps him, he has a sudden nose-bleed, staining the poem on the page; his undisguised tears in a rare moment of sincerity leads him to view the witness with hatred; his fond memories of the film, *Bengal Lancer*, are as juvenile as his constant recourse to angry threats.

The betrayal of Scobie originates in the lost childhood of Wilson. He had mastered what Pinkie was only learning: lying, bribery, blackmail, deceit. And the cruelest betrayal of all is his only too well-founded insinuation to the Pharisee Louise Scobie that her husband had committed suicide. Only Father Rank's belief in the mystery of God's ways ("Don't imagine you—or I—know a thing about God's mercy") can undo that betrayal and lead Louise to acknowledge that Scobie had loved no one else except God. The implicit analogy with Judas' betrayal of Christ is really the heart of the matter. Scobie is a would-be Christ; his career of sacrifice would seem to be a true *imitatio,* were it not that he too is psychologically rather than mystically driven. He feels an adult-like pity towards children, rather than a Christ-like compassion. He will take pity and accept his own moral corruption because he sees even in adults a projection of his dead daughter, his only child, "who had died at school in England three years ago—a little pious nine-year-old girl's face in the white muslin of first communion." And so when he finds an illegal letter to a daughter in Germany in the toilet of the ship Esperança, he not only sees the Captain as a father like himself but metamorphoses him into a child in his mind's eye:

> The man had lowered his bulk onto the edge of the bath as though it were a heavy sack his shoulders could no longer bear. He kept on wiping his eyes with the back of his hand like a child— *an unattractive child, the fat boy of the school.* Against the beautiful and the clever and the successful one can wage a pitiless war, but not against the unattractive: then the millstone weighs on the breast (italics mine).

Scobie will not turn in the illegal letter. The next stage in his downfall, a foreshadowing of future suicide, is his trip across a Styx-like river to view the body of a dead district commissioner who had been deeply in debt:

> When Scobie turned the sheet down to the shoulder he had the impression that he was looking at a child in a night shirt quietly asleep: the pimples were the *pimples of puberty and the dead face seemed to bear the trace of no experience beyond the class-room or the football field.* "Poor child," he said aloud (italics mine).

Scobie, too, will contract debts to Yusef the Arab merchant to send his wife to haven in South Africa. Pemberton's suicide note to "Dad" ("It was like a letter from school excusing a bad report") will lead to Scobie's own deception in his diary. Even his adulterous love affair with Helen Rolt confuses passion with pity. She, too, is a reincarnation of his dead daughter, as he first sees her clutching a stamp album "from her loving father on her fourteenth birthday." Scobie brings her presents of stamps (his spilling gin on a stamp anticipates Wilson's nose-bleed on the poem), and shortly before he kisses Helen for the first time, he sees her as ugly, "with the temporary ugliness of a child." Her love letter to Scobie, reminiscent of Pemberton's suicide note, only confirms Scobie's mistaken impression:

> *My dear my dear leave me if you want to or have me as your hore if you want to.* He thought: She's only heard the word, never seen it spelt: they cut it out of the school Shakespeares.

It is Scobie's inability to treat Helen as anything but the schoolgirl "who excells at net-ball" that will lead him to disaster. After she has denounced him for only taking pity, never loving, Scobie feels impelled to write a letter to Helen "the adult":

> How much older she is than she was a month ago. She hadn't been capable of a scene then, but she had been educated by love and secrecy: he was beginning *to form her* .... *In my school,* he thought wearily, *they learn* bitterness and frustration and how to *grow old* (italics mine).

His written declaration of love will be stolen and then used to blackmail him. But its most important consequence is to lead him to suspect his houseboy Ali of having betrayed him to Yusef and Wilson.

Scobie's complicity in the retributive death of Ali marks the penultimate station in his calvary of theological corruption. Here too children's faces provide psychological evidence. Along with Helen Rolt and the little boy to whom Scobie told his tale of a Judas-like betrayal, one other rescued passenger from the torpedoed boat attacts his attention. A little six-year-old girl for whose distraction Scobie makes shadow-pictures on the wall becomes in his mind's eye the image of his own dead daughter ("he saw a white communion veil over her head: it was a trick of the light on the pillow and a trick of his own mind"). He utters a self-sacrificing and Christ-like prayer: "Give her peace. Take away my peace for ever, but give her peace." I have discussed in Chapter II the device of the answered prayer to implicate the supernatural as motivating force in "realistic" novels. Here too the prayer will be answered, since in consequence Scobie's movement toward suicide and damnation soon becomes manifest. But in many ways more important in hastening his suicide is the death of Ali. At the very moment that he is about to cross the Styx into the world of Pemberton's suicidal death, Scobie dreams a dream which defines Ali's symbolic role in the novel as a pagan child of *before* the Fall:

> He was walking through a wide cool meadow with Ali at his heels: there was nobody else anywhere in his dream, and Ali never spoke. Birds went by far overhead, and once when he sat down the grass was parted by a small green snake which passed onto his hand and up his arm without fear and before it slid into the grass again touched his cheek with a cold friendly remote tongue.

Looking into the rearview mirror, Scobie sees Ali "nodding and beaming" (part of the edenic vision where snakes are friendly). Ali seems to represent that reflection of innocence in Scobie's soul (as did the children in Mauriac's *Vipers Tangle* discussed in Chapter II). Scobie thinks "that this was all he needed of love or friendship," but Ali will die, a victim of Scobie's pity for Helen's disdain of his pity. When one can suspect innocence of betrayal one has truly been corrupted. And Scobie will find his way "quickly and unhesitatingly to the body as though he had himself chosen the scene of the crime." Ali thus becomes, for a moment, Christ the victim, his body lying coiled like the image of God coiled at the end of Scobie's broken rosary (he had given that rosary to Ali as a token of identification to his murderers). "O God, I've killed you." Scobie says in a deliberately ambiguous prayer (Is God an expletive or the object of the verb?). The death of Ali will fuse with that of his daughter in Scobie's diary: "*Ali found murdered.* the statement was as plain and simple as that other time when he had written: *C. died.*" And the mendacious entries that will follow transform that former vehicle of self-knowledge into a log-book of the journey toward suicide and damnation: "O

God, I offer up my damnation to you. Take it. Use it for them."
This prayer, too, will be answered.

It is ironic that a character who sees virtually everyone as a pitiable child should be himself deprived of childlike traits by a not totally pitiless author who lavishes a not inconsiderable amount of affection on him. Perhaps this very absence constitutes Scobie's fall from grace. Certainly, one of the most successful effects created by *The Heart of the Matter* is that of Scobie's age and weariness, like the rusty handcuffs and the broken rosary. But Greene's art is too consistent to deny Scobie completely. The most convincing emblem of Scobie's corruption in death is, characteristically, taken from juvenile fiction:

> That night he dreamed that he was in a boat drifting down just such an underground river as his boyhood hero Allan Quartermain had taken toward the lost city of Milosis. But Quartermain had companions, while he was alone, for you couldn't count the dead body on the stretcher as a companion. He felt a sense of urgency, for he told himself that bodies in this climate kept for a very short time, and the smell of decay was already in his nostrils. Then, sitting there guiding the boat down the midstream, he realized that it was not the dead body that smelt but his own living one. He felt as though his blood had ceased to run: when he tried to lift his arm it dangled uselessly from his shoulder. He woke, and it was Louise who had lifted his arm. She said, "Darling, it's time to be off."
> "Off?" he asked.
> "We're going to Mass together."

In the lost childhood of Judas Christ was betrayed. It is most appropriate that AE's poem was entitled *Germinal*, for the loss of childhood or its perversion is an organic process. Spiritually, this growth can in no way be considered as qualitatively progressive. On the contrary, as Scobie fully realized:

> Is it because here human nature hasn't had time to disguise itself? Nobody here could ever talk about a heaven on earth. Heaven remained rigidly in its proper place on the other side of death, and on this side flourished the injustices, the cruelties, the meannesses, that elsewhere people so cleverly hushed up. Here you could love human beings nearly as God loved them, knowing the worst.

Graham Greene's first penetration of the disguise and his first gropings toward faith came to him at "the School," as he told us in *The Lawless Roads.* It may have been a childhood lost and betrayed, the imagery of his fiction shows; but it was a past that remained forever present as a well-spring of his novelistic imagination, a past to be recaptured by the act of creating a fictional world that revealed Man as God loved him, knowing the worst.